UNHOLY SACRIFICES OF THE NEW AGE

UNHOLY SACRIFICES
OF THE NEW AGE

PAUL DEPARRIE AND MARY PRIDE

CROSSWAY BOOKS □ WESTCHESTER, ILLINOIS
A DIVISION OF GOOD NEWS PUBLISHERS

Linotronic® Typesetting by TRC Enterprises, 10871 Sunset Hills Plaza, St.
Louis, Missouri 63127.

Cover design: Britt Taylor Collins

Third printing, 1990

Printed in the United States of America.

Library of Congress Catalog Card Number 88-704953

ISBN 0-89107-482-1

TABLE OF

Contents

FOREWORD

E very day the reports come in from across
America and around the globe—reports of
Satanic sacrifice, witchcraft rituals, murder,
and butchery.

Police in San Antonio, Texas are stunned by insistent reports
of child and animal ritual sacrifice.

According to reliable news reports, the environs of Los Angeles are littered with bones and debris from Satanic sacrifices.

In Dallas, law enforcement authorities gathered recently to
hear from experts on how to deal with teenage Satanic cults.

Officials of the United States Customs Services recently found
materials in a Tallahassee, Florida warehouse linked to a cult
group that uses children in demonic sex orgies.

In McComb, Mississippi, hysteria broke out this year as the
police were inundated with hundreds of phone calls from frantic
parents begging the authorities to protect their children from the
local Satanists' threats of child and baby sacrifice.

In Oklahoma a seventeen-year-old heavy metal rock fan
joined a teen devil cult where he willingly drank animal and

human blood—and wound up massacring both his parents as a sacrifice to his master, Lucifer.

These are obvious signs of the growing kingdom of Satan. *But another, even more sinister, movement towards pagan sacrifice* is now developing at terrific speed, unopposed and even encouraged by the police, judges, and the media.

In *Unholy Sacrifices of the New Age,* Paul deParrie and Mary Pride expose the powers of darkness that now operate in relative secrecy on so many fronts. They lay bare the surprising new modern movement towards cannibalism, ritual sacrifice, and ritual suicide, and its fraudulent claims that death is exciting, adventurous—even rewarding. The authors show how society is being desensitized to pain and suffering and being taught new pagan values devoid of mercy and empathy.

What a shocking and scary—but extremely important—book this is! It is a gripping and breathtakingly spectacular account of the darkness and evil that have taken a stranglehold on our society today. As the authors themselves conclude, "The ground has *already* been prepared for a mass sacrifice to the new gods . . . The first breaker of the New Wave is already sweeping over its victims." A whole generation is coming to love and desire death and to worship the destroyer.

Humanity is fast reaching a crucial time of decision. Neither you nor I can escape this crossroads. The question is, "Whom will you serve—Jesus Christ or the devil?" Will you accept the free gift of eternal life offered by the One who died for your sins and shed His blood for you on the cross? Or instead, will you choose to join the legions of the damned—the men and women who refuse God's perfect gift? Will you live joyously for all eternity, or will you, too, become an *unholy sacrifice of the New Age?*

Texe Marrs
Austin, Texas

Introducing Unholy Sacrifice

Sacrificial drums throbbed insistently in the heavy twilight air.

Straggling up the hill behind the village came the members of the tribe. At their head, the aged witch doctor carried the tokens of his office: some magical herbs wrapped in a large leaf and the sacrificial knife.

Behind him in the procession, tonight's victim was supported by several stout men.

He was young, healthy, and drunk.

At the top of the hill, the worshipers spread out in a circle around a rude stone altar. Sitting down with a gentle wheeze on a handy stone, the witch doctor commanded his followers to bind the young man to the altar.

He then led the group in a dance.

Weird chanting filled the air as the dance moved more swiftly around the altar. Drunk as he was, the young man on the altar knew what was coming.

He did not resist.

Unshocked, the onlookers watched as the knife did its deadly work. . . .

After the feast, the tribe members came back down the hill. They were in festive mood, chattering gaily. Not one dropped a tear over the fate of the young man whose bloody body, now minus certain essential organs, still lay limp on the altar.

He had served a useful purpose.

The goddess was pleased.

The harvest this year would be good.

Putting an end to scenes like that one . . . and scenes even more fearful, where the screams of children rent the air as their own parents handed them over for torture and death . . . was one of the first great earthly accomplishments of the religion of Jesus Christ.

Christianity's triumph over paganism was so complete, in fact, that Christians soon forgot what the pagans really believed and what kind of people they really were.

The Bible tells us that people once worshiped Baal and Molech and Ashtoreth and Chemosh.

It tells us that the people who performed this worship were "abominable" and that the Lord hated that kind of worship.

It tells us that the Lord had driven the unholy sacrifices, and the people who offered them, out of His land . . . and that when His own people took up this kind of sacrificing, He utterly refused to forgive them for it.

Guess what?

Baal is back.

And Molech.

And Ashtoreth.

And all the rest.

You have read about them in the newspapers and heard about them on TV.

But you probably have not recognized them, because today they do not look at all like the pictures in our old Sunday school workbooks.

❦   ❦   ❦   ❦   ❦

Today, this very minute, human torture and sacrifice is being planned or is occurring somewhere in the United States of America and around the Western world. Don't look for it in the back room of a shuttered house, with wild-eyed cult members circling around a smoking altar (although that is coming back, too). Look for it where you don't expect it . . . where respectable men and women gather together to plan a glorious future for humanity . . . a glorious future that, unfortunately, demands sacrifices.

Unholy sacrifices.

PART I: THOSE OLD-TIME RELIGIONS

ONE

Pagan Sacrifice in the Old Age

I desire mercy, not sacrifice.
(The Lord God as reported in Hosea 6:6)

*The custom of human sacrifice admits that the life of one
is taken to save the lives of many, or that an inferior
individual is put to death for the purpose of preventing
the death of somebody who has a higher right to live. . . .
Ritual killing often thrived in remote continents only
until it was extirpated by people who were Christians.*
(Nigel Davies, *Human Sacrifice in History and Today*)[1]

The Mongol officer and his companions rode
warily across the huge plain. He felt sure evil
had been stalking them. Three times suspicious
groups of men had offered to ride with him, but each time he and
his butler and groom had refused their services. Now they were
alone, far from home and help.

Just as the officer was congratulating himself on having
escaped the snares laid for him, his attention was gripped by the
sight of a group of fellow Muslims huddled around the body of a
dead companion by the side of the road. They were wailing heart-
breakingly and looked so forlorn that he reined in his mount and
asked what was their trouble.

One of the Muslims told him that they were soldiers far from
home who had been toiling hard in the Mongol service. The dead
man, sole provider for a large family, had died unexpectedly on the

road, due to the rigors of the journey. But, oh misery, none of them were educated men! None knew the funeral service in the holy Koran, and consequently they had no way of giving their friend a proper burial. Would the great captain condescend to say the funeral ritual for them? He would surely be blessed for it in both this world and the next.

Agreeing, the captain alighted and removed his weapons. After purifying himself with water, he knelt down on the carpet provided and piously recited the funeral ritual. One Muslim soldier knelt on each side of him. The butler and groom were a little way off, at the request of the other soldiers, so as not to distract their master's attention from the solemn proceedings.

Suddenly a signal was given. The "soldiers" swept out yellow handkerchiefs, threw them around the necks of the unsuspecting Mongols, and quickly strangled all three. In just a few minutes the officer and his companions were all dead and laid out according to the sacrificial ritual—sides gashed to keep their bodies from swelling, legs doubled back, and head to feet of the next body.[2]

The unfortunate captain and his companions were the victims of a particularly brutal cult, the Thugs. Dedicated to the worship of Mother Kali, this group flourished in India up until the time of the British Raj. In honor of an encounter between the Mother Goddess and some demons, whom she vanquished by garotting, the Thugs preyed on unsuspecting travelers. They did not kill for money or revenge, but for purely religious motives, as many Thugs took pains to make plain when captured. No, their ritual murders were genuine sacrifices to the goddess.

Human Sacrifice Then

Throughout human history, unholy sacrifice has taken many forms.

The Khonds of India raised special people, called Meriahs, to sacrifice to the Earth Goddess in their rituals, which consisted of killing the victim as slowly as possible: sometimes by cutting him to pieces while he lived, sometimes by forcing him to roll up and down on a stage while he was slowly burned to death. The Meriahs were encouraged to breed before they were sacrificed, and their children in turn were set apart for sacrifice.

The Aztecs, often praised as a "sophisticated civilization," had a standard way of dispatching their victims: cutting out their beating hearts. They varied this by drowning some, burning others alive, cutting the heads off of others, while the most unfortunate were first thrown into the fire, then pulled out to have their hearts cut out. Children were frequently sacrificed, as were women, slaves, and prisoners of war. Afterwards, sometimes the victims' bodies were eaten, with special emphasis on the vital organs: heart, liver, intestines, and brain.

Fiji cannibals not only ate human flesh, but went out of their way to torture the victims beforehand. Common was the boiling alive of the sacrificial victim. At other times a victim's arms and legs would be cut off, baked, and eaten before his own eyes. Neither young nor old was spared, and a man could even eat his own wife for no other reason than that he wanted to.

Right here in North America, Indian tribes vied with one another in inventing tortures for their sacrificial victims, including women and children. The Yamassees of what is now called Georgia were accomplished in these "arts."

> Some they cut to pieces slowly, joint by joint, with knives and tomahawks; others they buried up to the neck, then stood away at a little distance, and aimed arrows at their heads. As a further variant, they bound prisoners to a tree and pierced the tenderest parts of their naked bodies with sharp-pointed stakes of burning wood. [3]

An eyewitness account of how the Shawnee of Kentucky sacrificed a white captive in 1759 includes all the following:

> Applying brands, embers, and hot metal to various parts of body; putting hot sand and embers on scalped head; hanging hot hatchets about neck; tearing out hair and beard; firing cords bound around body; mutilating ears, nose, lips, eyes, tongue, and various parts of the body; searing mutilated parts of the body; biting

or tearing out nails; twisting fingers off; driving skewers in finger stumps; pulling sinews out of arms.[4]

Child sacrifice and infanticide were staples of pagan sacrifice. Often combined with cannibalism, these were considered, as one writer puts it, "basic to religion and essential for the survival of society."[5] In one close-knit group, status was based entirely on one's devotion to killing one's own children. These people, the Arioio in Tahiti, vowed to kill all of their children as sacrifices to their god. If an Arioi chanced, on getting older, to mellow into sparing one of his children, he became a second-class citizen.

Children and young people were made into medicines.[6] Children were also sacrificed to ensure future fertility.[7] Sometimes the children of the poor were killed in hopes that this would help the wife of a nobleman conceive.[8]

The extent and gruesomeness of unholy sacrifice varied from tribe to tribe and nation to nation. Those nations particularly adept in torture of their own people include the Indians (of India), who "showed an inventive genius rare in other lands,"[9] and the Aztecs and Mayans of Mexico. In other cultures, victims had to be from outside the tribe. The Indians and Mexicans, however, both stressed the belief that the victim would profit from his own sacrifice, thus allowing the executioner to feel no guilt and denying the victim the opportunity to protest his own sacrifice. As Nigel Davies, author of *Human Sacrifice in History and Today,* puts it,

> The underlying conditions did not alter: lack of any benevolent redeemer, absence of a truly humane ethic, and, finally, belief in a ceaseless cycle of rebirth that turned the death of man into a trivial incident.[10]

. . . And Human Sacrifice Now

Where these conditions prevail, pagan sacrifice goes on, even today. The members of Wycliffe Bible Translators, for example, often encounter the reality of pagan sacrifice in the course of their work. A recent issue of their magazine, *In Other Words,* tells the story of a baby named Zaccheus born in the Tharaka tribe in Meru district in Kenya. He was born premature, still surrounded with his bag of waters, and therefore taboo. His anguished mother was about to cast him into the cattle pen to be trampled under the cattle's hooves, as ritual demanded, when to everyone's surprise the husband's other wife grabbed the baby and ripped open the sac imprisoning him. Zaccheus began to cry, thus proving he was "alive" according to Tharaka definition, and his astonished mother received her baby as one raised from the grave. This very child, now a young man, has just become the Christian language helper for missionaries translating the Bible into the Tharaka language.[11]

Christianity Overcomes Sacrifice

As we read the story of Zaccheus, our natural reaction is to assume that, now that missionaries are in the tribe, such infant sacrifice will end. After all, everywhere else the Christian religion has spread, pagan sacrifice has ended. Anthropologists and researchers note this almost casually, as does Garry Hogg in his book *Cannibalism and Human Sacrifice,* in which he points out, "The practice of eating human flesh was noted in almost every part of the world, except Europe, as a recognized ingredient of the acceptable social order."[12] Hogg doesn't stop to ask or answer *why* Europe was spared from cannibalism, but the answer is obvious—Europe had been Christianized. Before the Christian missionaries came, the barbarous white tribes of Europe glutted themselves on human flesh and practiced ritual sacrifice as much as anyone else.

Back to Unholy Sacrifice

Today we are told that the progression away from sacrifice and torture of other human beings was a simple evolutionary phenomenon, caused by man's innate drive to better behavior. As we left behind bad environments, so the story goes, man's innate goodness has surfaced, and so now we have firmly left human sacrifice in the past—no thanks to Christianity. Our world is a pragmatic, secular, pluralistic world in which no religious act like pagan sacrifice could possibly occur.

This book will show that the opposite is true. As Western-ers—Americans, Australians, Canadians, English, French, Germans, and so on—have bought the idea that kindness and mercy flow automatically from a God-denying secular culture, we are being caught up in a new flood of unholy sacrifices. These sacrifices spare neither the young nor the old; neither women nor children; neither the innocent nor the helpless—as you will see for yourself.

Davies' "underlying conditions" for human sacrifice are again emerging in the West: "lack of any benevolent redeemer" and "absence of a truly humane ethic." Following hard on the heels of these conditions is the increasing "belief in a ceaseless cycle of rebirth that turned the death of man into a trivial incident."[13] Should this unholy trinity of values again erupt in full, as we will show is a real danger, Christians, as "enemies of the tribe," can expect the same treatment as the victims of the Mayans, Aztecs, Indians, and Fijians.

This should not come as a real surprise. Bible prophecy tells us that Satan's kingdom grows along with the Kingdom of God, and that Christians can expect "perilous times" when the church suddenly finds herself facing an outbreak of the old pagan religion of Babylon. Scripture also tells us that our job is to be faithful in such times, and that even when the final apostasy of the Antichrist arises, God will provide His church with an eternal sanctuary—provided we are faithful to Him.

T W O

Power in the Blood

Would you be free from the burden of sin?
There's pow'r in the blood . . . pow'r in the blood.
Would you o'er evil a victory win?
There's wonderful pow'r in the blood.

(From the famous hymn,
"There is Power in the Blood")

For Christ died for sins once for all, the righteous for the unrighteous, to bring you to God. (I Peter 3:18)

"The Khonds are keeping men and women as we keep pigs. They raise and fatten them until the time comes for a sacrifice. Then the victims are cut to pieces while alive, and their flesh offered to the Earth Goddess. These victims, called Meriahs, are allowed to marry and have children, who themselves become victims in their turn."

This information, submitted to the British government in 1836 by George Russell of the Madras, India, Civil Service, caused deep agony of soul in James Thomason, governor of the North-West provinces. Thomason, the son of a missionary and a devout Christian, was required by British law to refrain from converting the native Indians, which included a policy of non-interference in their religious rites. But could so gross an outrage against the laws of God as human sacrifice wait for the slow, leavening effect of British culture? Could he allow men, women, and children to be murdered painfully while waiting for a "better day" when the people would be more willing to listen to a foreign message?

9

Thomason wept, wavered, and finally sent a Major Campbell to "investigate" the reports of Meriah sacrifice.

Campbell did not share the governor's waverings. He was not concerned that he was going alone into villages filled with thousands of Indians, any of whom might quite possibly murder him if he outraged their gods. He called together the Khond chiefs and leaders, whom he had led in the war against the late rajah, and began to reason with them. First, he informed them that the "Great Government," meaning the British Raj, abhorred human sacrifice, and that under British law a life was required for a life. Making his meaning clear, Campbell threatened that those who sacrificed the Meriahs could be considered simple murderers and would be treated as such if they kept up this evil practice. The Khonds then suggested a compromise: only offering one Meriah per year for a whole group of villages. Campbell rejected this idea. He then asked the assembled leaders if they could show any proof that these sacrifices actually helped their crops prosper more than those of other tribes that did not commit human sacrifice.

Campbell was kept waiting for a while on pins and needles while the chiefs talked things over. Finally they returned with an answer. Since they were now subjects of the Great Government, they had to obey the law. If the goddess became upset, they would blame the British for the lack of sacrifices and tell her to pour her wrath on them.

And so it was done. The Khonds brought in the Meriahs, and Major Campbell went on working in the region for another sixteen years, during which time he rescued the amazing total of 1506 intended Meriah victims . . . bought or bred before his arrival.[1]

Confronting Baal

Thank God for Major Campbell . . . and for the tens of thousands of Christian missionaries, merchants, soldiers, and others who through the centuries fought human sacrifice and prevailed.

In this one story we see several features common to all successful encounters between Christians and the practitioners of human sacrifice.

(1) Major Campbell at least potentially sacrificed himself. He put his own life on the line to save the lives of others.

(2) Major Campbell had absolutely no vested interest in saving the Meriahs. He did not plead for them because he was concerned for himself. For example, he was not worried that if the Khonds kept on sacrificing Meriahs sooner or later they would start sacrificing Scottish majors.

(3) He laid down the law as *right*. He did not just say, "The government finds human sacrifice unhealthy and economically unsound." He informed the Khonds that the British found it disgusting and wrong.

(4) He took an absolute stand. Instead of settling for diminishing the number of Meriah sacrifices, he held out for stopping the sacrifices altogether.

(5) The major pointed out the consequences (in this case, temporal consequences) of continuing to sacrifice human beings. Although his own government had not dared to officially recognize religious sacrifice as murder, Campbell fearlessly took the position that, in future, this kind of murder would be treated as all other kinds of murder, and that therefore the Khonds would do well to abandon it voluntarily.

(6) Finally, Campbell did appeal to natural law. "Are your crops more blessed than the crops of other tribes that do not have Meriahs?" he asked the Khonds.

Substitute "the government of the Great God" for "the Great Government of the British" in the story of Major Campbell and the Khonds, and you have a pretty fair picture of how Christians have always preached against human sacrifice. These Christians of the past said human sacrifice was *wrong*, *an offense to God* which *He would punish*, that it absolutely must *totally stop*, and that further-more *they themselves would risk their own lives* to stop it. Some-times the missionaries went farther, like Campbell, and pointed out that the sacrifices did no real good. Other times their Biblical argu-ments alone were sufficient to abolish human sacrifice in a tribe. In all cases, eventually the Christians were victorious. Human sac-rifice and cannibalism ended.

Created in the Image of God

The first part of the powerful message that ended human sacrifice can be found right at the beginning of the Bible.

> So God created man in his own image,
> in the image of God he created him;
> male and female he created them. (Genesis 1:27)

This doctrine that man was created in the image of God made it impossible for one group of men to deny humanity to any other group. Since so much pagan sacrifice depended on considering the victim as non-human (thus the practice of calling victims "long pig" in New Guinea or "fish" in Fiji), restoring the victim's humanity automatically exempted him from sacrifice in such cases.

Missionaries also stood against another common pagan prac-tice—labeling some people as "children of the demons." In one tribe, for example, if a woman gave birth to twins, only one was considered to be the husband's, while the other was thought to be conceived from a demon. Handicapped or deformed babies were also commonly labeled "demon children," making it easy to justify killing them.

Horrified by this murder of helpless babies, Christian mission-aries preached that *every* descendant of Adam, whether black or white, pretty or deformed, healthy or unhealthy, inherits the "image of God" from Adam. Missionaries and native believers would take in these labeled children, if necessary.

So common were these works of charity, and so routinely did missionaries put themselves out to protect the unlovely, that they aroused the ire of latter-day eugenicists like Margaret Sanger, founder of Planned Parenthood, whom we shall meet in a later chapter. Sanger, echoing the original pagans, promoted the idea of killing off such "human weeds"—an idea we shall see in action later in this book.

The Life of the Flesh Is in the Blood

Some types of pagan sacrifices depended on redefining death. Zaccheus, the Tharaka man almost thrown to the cattle as a baby, was considered "dead" by Tharaka definition simply because he was born inside his bag of waters. Another instance of redefined death occurs in the Wycliffe film *Mountain of Light,* where a woman delirious with a high fever was buried alive in the sight of the missionaries because the spirit of those afflicted in this way supposedly departed while their bodies continued to breathe and even, as in this case, speak and groan.

In most cases, of course, the executioners of human victims did not much greatly care whether their victims were alive or dead, except to somewhat prefer living victims to torture. However, when the proposed victim was a tribe member, the definition of death did matter. The Biblical teaching that "the life of the flesh is in the blood" (Leviticus 17:11, 14) allowed the missionaries to see that the breathing person with his blood circulating really was *not* dead, thus leading them to intervene.

This teaching of bodily life as defined by a circulating supply of living blood has important consequences for today, as we shall see later on.

He Died and Was Buried

Why did Christian missionaries never learn to accept the pragmatic reasons offered for human cannibalism? Because from one end of the Bible to the other it is made plain that dead people are to be *buried,* not eaten or otherwise exploited by men. The book of Ecclesiastes goes so far as to say,

> A man may have a hundred children and live many years; yet no matter how long he lives, if he cannot enjoy his prosperity and *does not receive proper burial,* I say that a stillborn child is better off than he. (Ecclesiastes 6:3)

Out of the hundreds of Biblical references to death, almost universally "he died" is followed by "and was buried." The exception, the law for exposing criminals guilty of capital offenses on a tree, required that the body be buried "the same day" (Deuteronomy 22:23). Even the bodies of enemies slain in battle after having blasphemed the God of Israel were not to be exploited by men. In most cases they were buried. In the rest, God Himself devoted the bodies to "the birds of the air and the beasts of the field," thus ruling out the possibility that the Israelites, like almost all the other nations, could legitimately harvest the dead bodies for food or other reasons.

The dead in the Old Testament were unclean. Anyone who touched a dead person had to purify himself afterwards. The high priest was not even allowed to defile himself by touching the dead body of his nearest and dearest. This made it impossible to consider taking part of the dead person within oneself, whether as food, as surgical injection, or as medicine.

The Blood of the Innocent

The southern kingdom of Judah survived many rebellions against God, but finally committed the sin God would not pardon. His own people "filled Jerusalem with innocent blood," and so He thrust them out of His presence. One-third died of starvation and plague, another third were killed by the sword, and the tattered remainder shuffled off to Babylon as slaves.

Why did the residents of Judah murder the innocent? Because they had rejected the religion of Yahweh and taken up the rituals of the surrounding pagans.

One distinguishing feature of human sacrifice, as practiced by the Israelites and others, has always been that the innocent were just as likely, if not more so, to suffer than the guilty. Children, in particular, were prized as sacrifices *because* of their innocence, which made them more acceptable to the gods.

In recent times Christians have disagreed about whether the Bible still allows or requires capital punishment for those guilty of the crimes listed in the Old Testament: rape, murder, and so on. But all Christians have agreed that the Bible clearly teaches that the innocent are to be protected, not sacrificed. And even the guilty are not to be cannibalized or physically punished above and beyond the actual damage they have inflicted on another. There is *no* crime for which the Biblical penalty is cannibalism or ritual torture.

In fact, a fair definition of pagan sacrifice could be: "The murder, torture, and /or cannibalism of an innocent person justified as beneficial for himself, for another person or for society." Since the gods were offered sacrifices in order to benefit an individual or society as a whole, such sacrifices can be more or less "secular," depending on the relative fervor the worshipers feel for the gods or for the results of the sacrifice. The Fijians, for instance, are thought to have invoked the gods more as an excuse for their cannibal feasts than to have unwillingly feasted on humans in order to placate the gods. Such sacrifices are pagan, according to the Bible, even when those offering the sacrifices are tired of them (Isaiah 57:10). What counts is that the sacrifices are *made* and *justified*.

Thus, capital punishment is not a sacrifice because the victim is presumably not innocent. Neither is the killing of soldiers in wartime, or the accidental killing of civilians. Simple murder also does not count as human sacrifice, unless the murderer tries to cover up his real motives (greed, revenge, or whatever) by justifying the murder as serving some beneficial purpose. What sets sacrifice apart is that murder is called "good" and the victim is innocent.

Keep this definition in mind. It will come in handy later on.

One Sacrifice for All

How did the missionaries persuade pagans to give up the rituals that for thousands of years had been thought absolutely necessary to the tribe's survival?

Missionary John Beekman's example could stand for many others. Speaking to his corps of native evangelists, Mr. Beekman said,

> When people tell you the witch doctor sacrifices in order to bring about good health, agree with them. Tell them the witch doctor is right. Sacrifice *is* necessary, but don't stop there. Tell them the way to receive health and control of the spirit world is not through the witch doctor's sacrifice of chickens. Ask them where the witch doctor first got this idea about sacrifice; they won't be able to tell you. Then say, "Here in God's book it tells us that many centuries ago sacrifices took place because God told his people to do this until Jesus Christ was sacrificed. Now that Jesus has been sacrificed for man's sin, it is no longer necessary for the witch doctor to do this."[2]

John Beekman was dealing with the question of animal sacrifice, but his advice can easily be applied to human sacrifice. The preacher then would simply inform his hearers that God had never required human sacrifice, only animal sacrifice, but that even animal sacrifice had been made obsolete by the sacrifice of Jesus Christ on the cross.

Any pagan could understand that a greater sacrifice replaced a lesser. This is the teaching that swept human sacrifice from the pagan world, not (as humanists would have it) the "modern" doctrine that there is no God and therefore no need for sacrifices. An outbreak of Christianity, not an outbreak of atheism, paved the way for the abolition of unholy sacrifice.

Service as Sacrifice

Another pagan doctrine remained to be dealt with. Tribes that sacrificed only outsiders did not concern themselves much with the state after death of those they dispatched. Those that killed their own members, however, had designed elaborate justifications for the victim's death.

The most powerful of these justifications, one that remains

today as part of Hindu, and now New Age, doctrine, is the combined dogma of karma and reincarnation.

Reincarnation literally means "fleshed again." It is the doctrine that after death we simply are born again as another person or
creature. This means you never really die; you just pass on to
another life.

Karma is the bad or good you store up for yourself in previous
lives. Everything that happens to you in this life is considered to
be a direct effect from something good or bad you did in a previous life. Everything you do in this life will also lead to good or bad
karma in future lives. Therefore, any suffering you receive is *your
own fault,* and not to be pitied. And since suffering patiently leads
to good karma in a future life, relieving pain is positively an evil
act.

Mix these doctrines with human sacrifice, and you end up with
victims who sincerely believe they will be benefited by being sacrificed, and executioners who feel positively noble about murdering
the victim. Also, since being sacrificed benefits the victim, there is
no theoretical limit on the number of executions. All other forms of
sacrifice had to justify some benefit to a third party or society. Only
karma/reincarnation makes *being* sacrificed the benefit.

This explains the incredible amount of sacrifice that went on
in both Hindu and Aztec civilizations. Both cultures strongly
stressed that people who submitted to sacrifice in this life would
receive a superior station in the next.

Strengthened by this belief in the personal benefits of his own
sacrifice,

> a man could be led to the sacrificial altar with the same air of
> indifference as if he were a goat. Europeans . . . were always
> amazed by the bemused calm with which the chosen victim faced
> his gruesome fate.[3]

In place of these bloody self-sacrifices, Christians preached
the self-sacrifice taught in the Bible: self-denial and service of others. Scripture, after all, uses this very language. It urges the believ-

er to present his body as a "living sacrifice" by serving God in every way and with all his strength (Romans 12:1, 2). "Accept the sacrifice of Jesus Christ, and do good in this world for greater blessing in the next" replaced "Suffer passively at the hands of others in this world for greater blessing in the next."

Once to Die, and After That the Judgment

Christianity also directly attacks the idea of infinite future lives, as well as the concept of an afterlife blessed because of sacrifice to pagan gods. According to the Bible, "It is given unto men once to die, and after that the judgment" (Hebrews 9:27). Hell awaits those who fail to seek reconciliation with the true God through the proffered sacrifice of His one and only Son.

The doctrine of Hell, so much despised in our day, gave missionaries a counterweight to the pagan doctrines of reincarnation and karmacized afterlives. The witch doctor told you that you would be cursed if you didn't go along with the pagan ways, including pagan sacrifice. Now the missionary tells you you will be cursed if you don't go along with the Christian ways, including giving up sacrifice. You then have to weigh the two doctrines for *truth*, since each promises similar consequences to those who deny it and those who accept it: misery or blessedness in the next life. And once truth becomes an issue, Christ, who is the Truth, can shine forth.

The Last Enemy

"The last enemy that shall be destroyed is death"(1 Corinthians 15:26).

Later on in this book we will see people arguing that death is a friend. Christians of the past, those who founded hospitals and poured billions of hours into medical research, did not agree. They fought death instead of surrendering to it. Why? Because the Bible clearly identifies death as an enemy.

The argument will be raised that in this verse God is speaking of spiritual death. We agree, the verse speaks of spiritual death . . .

but God is also speaking of physical death. In this case the two cannot be separated. The context of this verse is a discussion of resurrection, and the part of man that is resurrected is his body.

Believers have long identified death as an enemy. We know we do not remain in a spirit form forever, but are clothed with a physical, though immortal, body after the resurrection. The early Christians also realized that a lax attitude towards death in one area would lead to the same in another area. The Platonic dualism of pre-Christian times became the Gnosticism that plagued the early church and often still troubles us. These heresies teach, essentially, that physical life is unimportant while spiritual life is everything. Scripture completely opposes this kind of thinking. Repeatedly God demonstrates that human, physical life is unique and deserves every protection, so much so that those who dare to take life unjustly show themselves unworthy of life of flesh *or* spirit.

It is true that physical life without spiritual life is going to result in spiritual death (not to mention physical death). But it is only during our physical lives that the option of life in Christ is available. Death will silence the praise of God that the world needs to hear.

"For in death there is no remembrance of thee: in the grave who shall give thee thanks?" (Psalm 6:5).

Death, *all* death, is God's enemy and our enemy. Sacrifice, *all* sacrifice except the sacrifice of Christ and the self-sacrifice of believers who serve God and man with our living strength, is likewise God's enemy and our enemy. He never made them a part of the Garden of Eden, and they won't even be remembered in the New Jerusalem.

THREE

It's Not Nice to Worship Mother Nature

The old tyrants invoked the past.
The new tyrants will invoke the future.

(G. K. Chesterton)

Both sacrificer and victim knew that the act was
required, to save the people from calamity and the cos-
mos from collapse. Their object was, therefore, more to
preserve than to destroy life.
(Nigel Davies, *Human Sacrifice in History and Today*)[1]

Human sacrifice. Torture. Cannibalism. Infanticide. Before the religion of Jesus Christ entered the non-Jewish world, these practices were common among the nations.

We today tend to think of these ancient pagans as superstitious, emotional folk indulging an animalistic lust for blood. Actually, many pagan societies were extremely complex and sophisticated. Think of Egypt, or ancient Babylon. In these societies, the priests, witch doctors, and astrologers were the learned men. They practiced human sacrifice and other gruesome rituals because they believed these practices were *necessary* and *effective* for the good of society and the good of its leaders.

The gods in these ancient societies often resembled "forces" more than people, and the more sophisticated in those societies regarded the gods as such. A god might stand for Fertility, or The

20

Change of Seasons, or Healing. Less sophisticated pagans might worship Mother Astarte; the elite worshiped only the virtues of sexual fulfillment, fertility, and success that she represented.

Primitive attempts to appease these gods seemed "scientific" to the pagans of the past. Witch doctors and pagan priests were laden with statistics, proofs, and anecdotal evidence of the efficacy of their rituals. They believed that there was a cause-and-effect linkage between offering the sacrificial victim and better crops, better health, or victory against opponents.

It's Not Nice to Worship Mother Nature

When an ancient society practiced human sacrifices and cannibalism, most often these practices were connected with the worship of "the goddess."

The goddess, Mother Earth, represented the beauty, harmony, and especially the fertility of nature. Her powerful association with spring rites and all the attendant flowers, dancing, and music has left the image of a very motherly goddess. However, strong sexual overtones were included in the ceremonies; temple prostitution was an important element in her worship. And though her worshipers were allowed to celebrate the new life of spring, even then the goddess sought blood in exchange for her blessing of reviving nature. If she stood for beauty, she also stood for evil and cruelty: the death of plants in autumn, the unforgiving aspect of nature in culling the weak. This side of the goddess needed to be appeased as well.

The creative deity of the universe was regarded in a number of religious systems from earliest times as a Mother Earth, a fertility goddess, carved or modeled with generous breasts and ample haunches, giving promise of the full measure of earth's abundance. Through the ages this mother goddess developed several subsidiary aspects besides the nourishing and maternal being who was the universal provider. These aspects became separately personified and were worshipped as varying manifestations of the great deity. Frequently she was a sex goddess, a courtesan or divine harlot. Sometimes she was the goddess of illicit love; sometimes the devoted spouse, or spotless virgin.

But there was yet another face, an awe inspiring image typifying the deep-seated dread aroused by the unpredictable hazards of man's existence. This dire concept of woman recurs in mythologies the world over. The benign mother-protectress then emerges as a goddess of warfare, of the chase, of pestilence, of blood sacrifice and death, and among the other manifold terror-shapes which invest the primordial and mysterious Female in man's mind. As such she stands for the cruel, unpitying, avenging side of the cosmic process. In classical myth these qualities manifest as the child-stealing Lamia, The Harpy, the Gorgon and the Fury; in Tibetan Buddhism as the wrathful and destructive female demons. Hinduism has a host of such deities, but in none are these attributes more forcefully conceived than in the figure of the goddess Kali.

The name Kali means "black." She may be called the Indian counterpart of black deities who appear in the pantheons of several old religions. Ancient Egypt had a Black Isis, Rome had a Black Venus, and a Demeter Melaina, "Black Demeter," was the Greek version of the dark-visaged goddess.

But Kali probably takes precedence in the hierarchy of the black-hued deities because although her blackness may ultimately be due to her tropical, aboriginal inheritance, she is in essence Blackness personified, ruling over all the dark elements of Nature.[2]

Whether known as Kali (the many-armed Hindu goddess Kali, who wears for a necklace a chain of human skulls), Diana, Isis, or Astarte, Mother Earth or her dark mirror image consistently required blood as an appropriate offering; she who created (or procreated) also destroyed and devoured her own young in bloody ritual.

Such worship is not unknown in modern times. For instance, Kali is still worshiped with blood sacrifice in India. So powerful is her following in that land that, though India has outlawed blood sacrifice, sacrifice to Kali remains. While it is true that the only *legal* sacrifice is that of a goat, the policing of such regulations carries a very low priority in this much-troubled country. What is done surreptitiously is, of course, unknown but zealots are rarely restrained by mere human laws. Occasionally one still hears today about human sacrifices, as in the case of a fifteen-month-old girl who was drowned to guarantee pregnancy (with a boy) of a child-less woman. In this case the goddess Devi—the goddess of both evil and of the war against evil—was being honored.[3] Edith Schaeffer, widow of the great evangelical pastor and theologian Francis Schaeffer, also tells the tale of a young man who arrived at Swiss L'Abri after fleeing for his life from a group of Kali-worshipers. He had become entwined in this group, and was eagerly looking forward to the big sacrifice ritual that would make him a full member. The day before the ritual, much to his shock, he found out that he was slated to be the sacrifice![4]

In light of these things, the current revival of paganism and goddess worship is particularly troubling. Who can assure us that such practices have not and will not be revived with the cults that spawned them? And wouldn't such assurances be meaningless coming from people who have joined these groups, thus lending their approval to the rituals performed in the past?

Blood for the Earth

The revival of paganism today is largely the result of the emerging "New Age" movement. In his best-seller *Dark Secrets of the New Age,* author Texe Marrs tells us "There is now a modern-day revival of the worship of the Mother Goddess, especially by feminist New Agers . . . many in the New Age have actually begun to worship the Mother Goddess."[5]

Worshipers of the Earth-goddess are not being poetic when they call her "Mother" or "Gaia" and treat her like a person. They are convinced that this planet actually has a consciousness, a superior consciousness which is capable of receiving worship . . . and insult. Their view of the earth as a larger system which includes individual systems of human beings who depend on it makes it, in their eyes, worthy of worship.

This idea of planet-as-person is no longer confined to a small group of heavily stoned Californians. One of us was recently dumbfounded to find this quote highlighted inside a reverent cream-colored box in *Organic Gardening,* a large circulation magazine that formerly used to confine itself to ruminations on "Ten Great Tomatos for Your Garden":

> If food-sharing is the fountainhead and source of our original humanity then we most truly perform that humanity when we share food and see with Lewis Thomas in his *Lives of the Cell* that the whole earth is a single cell and that we are all simply symbiotic organelles involved with one another . . . The global politics that issues forth from this vision is truly a *bios* and a *logos.* [6]

So we all are just "symbiotic organelles" on the surface of the great Cell, Mother Earth. Not only that, the author of this quote (and evidently the editors of *Organic Gardening*) consider the cult of the Great Cell a *bios* and *logos. Bios* is Greek for "life." *Logos* is Greek for "word." Both are used as names for Jesus Christ and His gospel in the Greek New Testament. Thus, the cult of Mother Earth is *self-consciously* a new gospel.

It is worth noting that a large portion of New Agers are heavily concentrated in the environmental movement. Once we recognize this, we should see a whole new meaning to some of the things that environmentalists say. How will we now understand their intent when they claim that the use of Earth's mineral resources is "rape"? It is likely to be much more literal in their minds than we had previously imagined.

Many of the devotees of the goddess today are not hesitant to blame many of today's droughts, pestilences, earthquakes, and other Earth-related disasters on humanity's failure to properly worship her and our continued abuse of her bounty. An angered goddess, she is wreaking vengeance for being ill-treated.

Is it any surprise that organizations like Earth First! are willing to endorse anti-human practices like "spiking" merely to save a tree? Spiking is where huge nails are driven into trees in forests where eco-freaks wish to stop the cutting. The nails are practically invisible once driven in, and a chain saw striking one will break the chain and endanger the workers. The same danger appears when the trees are cut at the mill. Since the loggers do not know which trees are spiked, they are afraid to work in areas that have been spiked. New Age influences provide a basis for many types of action, from civil disobedience to sabotage, to "save" the Earth from people of "lower consciousness" . . . from insults to her person.

Will the goddess once again demand blood? Will she, according to her priests and followers, demand the life of the interloper?. . . the infidel?. . . the insolent?

A better question is: When has she not?

Mellow Fellows and Evolutionary Revolutionaries

Before we go any farther, we need to make something clear. Just as all that glitters is not always tinsel, so all that is labeled, or labels itself, "New Age" is not necessarily *religiously* New Age. Just like other religious movements, the New Age Movement is made up of two different strands of people: true believers and tag-alongs.

Nominal New Agers could be called "Mellow Fellows." These believe in living in harmony with God's creation, not in becoming slaves of an Earth Goddess. They prune their trees without first praying to them; they wipe out roaches without twinges of guilt. Some of them are semi-Christianized; others are straight pantheists; but all of them are interested more in a personally happy life than in grand dreams of cosmic progress. Tilling the soil on an Arkansas farm, or feeding the chickens in a California backyard, Mellow Fellows feel that progress towards cosmic union is inevitable and they don't have to particularly knock themselves out to help it along. They have no interest at all in sacrificing anybody else for some great Plan.

In family life, Mellow Fellows sometimes follow the larger society's "morals," but quiet often they are faithful husbands, wives, fathers, and mothers. They believe in health and harmony, so place high value on family games and homemade entertainment. Suspicious of high-tech medicine, they prefer home birth, breast-feeding, and alternative forms of medical care.

Mellow Fellows range from mildly socialistic to downright libertarian. Mostly they just want to be left alone and are willing to leave others alone in turn.

In many cases, most Mellow Fellows are New Agers simply because that is what everyone is in their particular subculture. It's "in" to be New Age, just like it once was "in" to be a Vietnam War protester. They may "meditate," but have no searing desire to contact unearthly spirits. Very likely they have never had serious contact with Bible-believing Christianity, so they equate Christianity with Big Government, Big Business, and Middle-Class Dress for Success, none of which they find appealing.

In short, Mellow Fellows are trying to be good people—without Christ. They are basically no more sinister than unsaved atheists and agnostics.

Evolutionary Revolutionaries are a different story. These are the True Believers who, while speaking of "cosmic harmony," actually despise the present created order of things. Their hearts ardently long for the next evolutionary jump forward—and they want to help it along. As you will see later in this chapter, these consider sacrifice and coercion to be *necessary* for progress. They are excited about contacting demon spirits (whom they call "Ascended Masters" or some similar title) and throw themselves fervently into neo-pagan rituals. Some are witches, some druids, some goddess-worshipers, some planet-worshipers.

Communists were a problem, but not a real threat, until Lenin invented his "Vanguard Doctrine," which said that a committed corps of communist believers could speed up the evolutionary process towards world communism. Until that time, communists had believed in Marx's doctrine of the inevitable evolutionary triumph of communism, and thus many were willing to let their cause triumph on its own. When Lenin seized power, he alienated many of these fellow-communists—all the more so when he unveiled his doctrine of the "Red Terror," which justified the slaughter of millions and presented communism as a continual terrorist revolution. Those who had naively longed for the future utopian "dictatorship of the proletariat" and who protested his brutality were the first to be executed.

Similarly, Christians need to be aware that not everyone called a "New Ager" is really hostile to human rights and God's revealed truth. Many are simply ignorant of the Bible and real Christian living. These Mellow Fellows quite often have real human concern for the unfortunate, and would be thoroughly disgusted to see any revival of unholy sacrifice. If any such revival broke forth, these, naively protesting like the true communists of Lenin's day, would likely be the first to be sacrificed.

When we speak of New Agers and the New Age Movement from now on, we will be speaking of the Evolutionary Revolutionaries—those who created and are promoting the New Age Vanguard Doctrine. But please understand that on the fringes of this movement are many who do *not* believe in the Vanguard Doctrine—just as many so-called Christians do not believe in really sacrificing themselves for the cause of Christ. These people are not religious New Agers, but cultural New Agers, just as among us we find cultural Christians. And *all* New Agers, just as all agnostics, atheists, nominal Christians, Muslims, and so on, are at least potentially reachable by the gospel. Jesus cast out demons in first-century Palestine. His followers today can do the same.

The New Wave: The Marriage of Science and Paganism

The New Age is actually not new. It started in Babylon, and will continue on until the end of this present world in fire as revealed in the book of Revelation. The only thing "new" about the New Age is its modern pseudo-scientific facade, centered around the religious doctrine of evolution.

Ancient Babylonian and Hindu beliefs included the doctrine of evolution. The goddess Kali was designated, among other things, the goddess of "becoming" or evolution. Reincarnation, the spiritual form of evolution, was part of both of these religions.

It is no surprise, then, to find New Age leaders trying to bring the old doctrines up-to-date by capitalizing on their "scientific" side. By this process they parasitize the existing humanist thinkers and institutions, assimilating their social respectability, power, and money into the New Age Movement. *This amalgamation of old-style humanism and Old Age paganism is the New Wave*—the New Agers' mechanism for social change.

New scientific hypotheses that man, as well as other species, may have made sudden and rapid transformations while evolving were initially proposed because scientists found, to their embarrassment, that the evidence for slow, gradual change just was not there. New Agers have transformed this teaching into the hope of an imminent "quantum leap" in the spiritual, mental, and physical condition of mankind. This, they announce, will cause society itself to evolve into a New Age.

"Non-Existence of the Unfit Has Been the Law of Nature"

Part of the process of change, New Agers believe, will come with the acceptance of "new" religious principles. Worship of Nature is one of the ancient pagan principles that New Agers think of as "new." Increasingly, they view Earth as a living entity who responds to worship.

Nature worship, unfortunately, is more than frolics in verdant groves and pentatonic pan pipes. Real acts of pagan worship have always required real sacrifices.

The pantheistic assertion that "God is everything and everything is God" leads quite naturally to the idea that we should not overburden the goddess (Earth) with superfluous and imperfect lower life forms such as the handicapped, or with people who insult her sensibilities by failing to worship her, such as Christians and Jews.

As noted transcendental meditation teacher Maharishi Mahesh Yogi sees it, Nature herself (Mother Earth) simply will not allow some people to live:

> There has not been and there will not be a place for the unfit. The fit will lead, and if the unfit are not coming along there is no place for them. . . . In the Age of enlightenment there is no place for ignorant people.
> Nature will not allow ignorance to prevail. It just can't. *Nonexistence of the unfit has been the law of nature*. (emphasis ours)[7]

This follows quite naturally from the teaching of the pre-Nazi "guru," doctor of law Karl Binding, who actually persuaded the

Germans to put this teaching into effect. Binding stated,

> As society progresses in a spiral, we will again come to see the higher morality of destroying the unfit.[8]

A wonderful future of peace, plenty, and happiness, New Age leaders say, awaits mankind at the dawning of the Age of Aquarius; an escape from the destructive, separatist evils of the Piscean Age with its rigid, unfeeling Christian religion. Back to the loving arms of Mother Earth, the goddess, for relief.

Two Races, Two Destinies

According to New Agers, the only thing holding back this planet-wide explosion of Luv is the presence of less developed (evolved) souls who are resisting the change. In their mythology, there are two kinds of people left from ancient times: the Atlantean and the Lemurian. Atlanteans are warlike and separatist. Lemurians, peaceful and caring, have a higher consciousness. New Age leaders claim their "messiah" has put off his return several times because of the Atlantean interference. Yet they believe their time is near and they work tirelessly toward it. For purposes of clarification, one should not confuse the Atlantean race of warlike people with the Atlantean times. Most New Agers hark back to these times with a fondness akin to older folks reminiscing about the "good old days."

New Age leaders feel it is important that they help awaken those who are capable of the evolutionary leap to godhood; but what is to be done with those who are unwilling or unable to jump? What did the Cro-Magnon man do with the Neanderthal? Now that *Homo sapiens* is being replaced by the *Homo noeticus* (new man) of New Age visionary Willis W. Harman, what criteria will be applied to distinguish between them?[9]

Leaders in the New Age Movement insist that the *Homo noeticus* will be a new race of people and that this new race will be recognized by several features. Ruth Montgomery, known as "The

Herald of the New Age," declares, "Those who survive the change will be a different type of people from those in physical form today."[10]

New Age groups teach the two-races concept in different ways, but all agree that some sort of higher or so-called "Christ" consciousness is an earmark of the new super-man. This is specifically the recognition that man is god, whereas lower consciousness insists that God is separate (holy) and distinct from the created order. Belief in a separate, personal (having His own personality) God is classified as "negative thinking," a sure sign of spiritual inferiority.

In other words, you and I are the lower, loser race if we believe in the God of the Bible. Revolutionary Evolutionary New Agers neither expect us nor particularly want us to survive "the change"—whatever that is—unless we join their camp. Instead of the Nazis' "Jewish problem," could this be the start of a "Christian problem"?

Science as Predator

Let us suppose that the evolutionists, New Age or humanist, are right. They would say that man needs a predator, someone to cull the weak in order to force mankind to the next step on the physical evolutionary plane.

Man himself is the only one intelligent enough, strong enough, ruthless enough to fill the predator's role. First, however, someone has to decide just what kind of humanity we should leap into; what traits, what aberrations, what qualities should mark some as survivors and others as evolutionary dead ends.

The first step on this road began with the introduction of eugenics teaching into the Christianized West.

Eugenics means "breeding for good genes," and eugenics schemes have been with us for thousands of years, from the ancient Greek republic of Sparta until now. They have always *sounded* logical, like breeding practices with animals. Christians knew better than to prey on the weak or deprive them of civil rights, though. Robert Malthus, a clergyman who in 1798 claimed that our problems stemmed from overpopulation among the poor, was the first really important supporter of eugenics in the Christian West.

Not too many Westerners were ready to follow Malthus until Darwin came along. It was not until this century that a dedicated group of individuals came together to "improve the race." Influential in America were Margaret Sanger, founder of Planned Parenthood; Lothrop Stoddard, one of Sanger's board of directors and author of a little dissertation entitled *The Rising Tide of Color Against White World Supremacy;* Dr. Ernst Reudin, the Nazi Eugenics Minister who also happened to be a personal friend of Sanger; and Dr. Carl Jung, famous psychiatrist who also reigned as judge in a Nazi eugenics court.[11]

"Sterilize All the Fundamentalists"

In 1924 the state of Virginia passed a compulsory sterilization law at the peak of a eugenics craze. The first person selected to be sterilized was eighteen-year-old Carrie Buck, an involuntary resident of the State Colony for Epileptics and Feeble- Minded. But some vocal Virginia Christians forcefully objected. These Christians insisted that even wards of the state had human rights and challenged the state's right to mutilate her. Eventually the case was lost and the alleged champion of civil liberties, Oliver Wendell Holmes, wrote the majority opinion. His good friend, Professor Harold Laski, a British socialist, wrote to praise his decision in Carrie Buck's case and ended his letter, "Sterilize all the unfit, *among whom I include all fundamentalists."* [12]

"Retarded by the Christian Way of Thinking"

The revelations of Nazi atrocities after World War II briefly set back the eugenics cause. However, no one should be under the mistaken impression that this business of sterilizing and killing off those judged to be defective was somehow a Nazi invention. The Germans had already bought into the evolutionary teachings of Nietzsche, Hegel, and others who preceded the Nazis. Even Margaret Sanger's ideas were fermenting in Teutonic minds long before the Nazi party was formed.

The most influential eugenics work of all time is *The Release of the Destruction of Life Devoid of Value*. This book was written by a prominent jurist (Karl Binding) and a noteworthy psychiatrist (Alfred Hoche) in 1920, years before Nazism. Binding and Hoche laid the foundation for all legal and medical justifications for mass murder of retarded and deformed people.

According to these distinguished, respectable men, only a distortion in our way of thinking—namely, Christianity—kept us burdened with the handicapped. Binding complained,

> A long and painful development over the centuries has been retarded partly because of the Christian way of thinking which has brought us to our present level of thinking.

> A new time will come when we no longer in the name of higher morality will carry out this demand that has its origin in an exaggerated idea of humanity.

> The present morality places too much value on mere continuation of existence and asks too high a sacrifice.[13]

German psychiatrists began exterminations *before* the Third Reich, and it was at the urging of the above-mentioned book that Nazi eugenicists took up the practice. In some cases the gassing facilities of a psychiatric hospital were dismantled only to be reconstructed for use in a Nazi death camp.[14]

Elimination of the unwanted was only the logical result of the evolutionary concept of culling the human herd.

Send the Unenlightened "Out of This World"

Humanistic evolution, however strongly believed, lacked a certain something at its core. It was entirely this-worldly, practical, unspiritual, unemotional. But today the ground prepared by rock-ribbed scientists has been taken over by spiritually-minded New Age leaders. Whereas the old humanist scientists believed in long, drawn-out evolutionary processes spanning millions of years, the

New Age believes in instant evolution. We are told that we create our own evolution, and that if enough of us are willing, we can all evolve in one giant leap forward.

New Age prophet Shirley MacLaine puts it this way: "Everything is working to the purposeful good. I don't care if someone mugs me on the street; I drew it to myself."[15]

Some cynic, hearing this, might wonder if the eight million victims of Josef Stalin's state-orchestrated famine "drew it to themselves"? Or, if "everything is working to the purposeful good," would it be acceptable to her for one of her followers to also be her mugger?

Fundamentalist Christians, who tend to think negative thoughts like this, do not seem to be among those that radical New Agers want to "draw" to themselves. And what to do with those troublesome Bible-thumpers and others who refuse to evolve spiritually when the New Age arrives? New Age spokesman Ken Eyers says,

> Those who cannot be enlightened will not be permitted to dwell in this world. They will be sent to some equally appropriate place to work their way to understanding.[16]

If you are not "in this world" you can only logically be out of it. In other words, you can only be dead. But if you believe in reincarnation, it's not hard to believe that killing someone doesn't really kill them. Supposedly murder just provides the victim with another chance to do life right. With this in mind, we suspect that this "equally appropriate place" is a mere six feet below this place.

Help Me Make It If I'm Right

New Age author, Moira Timms explains how the "right" people will be guided through the transformation,

> Spiritual preparedness is what is needed for ultimate survival . . .
> So let us state it very clearly: those who embody the consciousness of the New Age and are performing greater services to

humanity will receive divine protection . . . The good shepherds know their sheep and the light in the spiritual eye in the forehead identifies those on the journey home. The stormy channel from this age of sorrows cannot be navigated by life-forms of unrefined vibrations. This is the Law.[17]

In other words you will have to earn your existence by thinking like Timms ("embody the consciousness of the New Age") and by producing more than you consume ("performing greater services to humanity"). Guidance and protection will come, one must assume, from divine people like Timms; those good shepherds leading those with the "light . . . in the forehead" (perhaps shaped like a 666).

David Spangler, another New Age leader, is concerned to rehabilitate non-believers. Spangler insists that we will be sent to "inner worlds" only so we can "be contained and ministered to until such a time as [we] can be safely released into physical embodiment again."[18] Good of him . . . assuming he really *could* raise the dead, which he can't.

These are not the isolated statements of one man, but the general consensus of the key people in this world-wide movement.

It's Your Karma, Dear Susan

We sometimes wonder why people in ancient pagan societies put up with the sacrifice of their sons, daughters, wives, and even themselves. The answer is simple. The victims were told they would be *rewarded* by the gods in the next life for their sacrifice.

Here the New Age (actually, Old Age) doctrine of karma and reincarnation takes on a different meaning. Karma is more than a mere trendy California fad. Karma is actually a sophisticated way to eliminate mercy and pity from the world.

According to karma, you get what you deserve, and the more you suffer patiently, the better off you will be in the next life. Thus, anyone who rescues you from suffering and death is actually *harming* your chances in the next life. In the same way, refusing to be sacrificed will cause you endless grief in the next existence. Even your executioner can plunge the knife in with a clear conscience, knowing he is helping you into a better existence.

Christian author Frank Peretti explains this strikingly in a scene from his thrilling best-seller, *This Present Darkness*.

A very strange-looking, black-robed and beaded, long-haired little guru from some dark and pagan land stepped into Susan's room at Kaseph's bidding. He bowed in obeisance to his lord and master, Kaseph.

"Prepare the altar," said Kaseph. "There will be a special offering for the success of our endeavor."

The little pagan priest left quickly. Kaseph returned his attention to Susan.

"Stop that!" he shouted. "Stop that praying!"

The force of the blow nearly knocked her out of the chair, but one guard held her firmly. Her head sank and she began to sob in very short, shallow gasps of terror.

Kaseph, like a conqueror, stood above her and boasted over her limp and trembling form. "You have no God to call upon! With the nearness of your death you crumble, you fall back upon old myths and religious nonsense!"

Then he said, almost kindly, "What you don't realize is that I'm actually doing you a favor. Perhaps in your next life your understanding will be deeper, your frailties will have fallen away. Your sacrificial gift to us now will build wonderful karma for you in the lives to come. You'll see."

Then he spoke to the guards. "Bind her!"

They grabbed her wrists and held them behind her; she heard a click and felt the cold steel of the manacles. She heard herself screaming . . .

In the book Susan was rescued by angels (we didn't want you to worry!). But if Kaseph's beliefs become widespread, who in real life will rescue us?

Human Sacrifice as Social Concern

Today, some are beginning to say that pagan human sacrifice was not all bad. Nigel Davies, for example, ends his book *Human Sac-*

rifice in History and Today this way:

> Faced with the mass brutality of our century, real as well as simu-
> lated [here he means the faked killings on TV shows], one may
> ask whether, in its place, man might not do better to revert to the
> ritualized killings of the past . . .
>   Traditional society [he is referring to pagan society] catered
> for both material and spiritual needs; sacrifice and religious ritu-
> als . . . were a vital uniting force in the community. Human sacri-
> fice thus played its part in man's striving to live in harmony with
> the cosmos. Whilst rituals may vanish and beliefs change, the
> need seems no less urgent in our modern fragmented society for
> man to recover that lost sense of cohesion.[19]

At one point in Davies' book he says,

> The Chinese *Book of Rites* is quoted affirming that sacrifice . . .
> has as its main aim to bring back social union and to restore the
> cosmic order. [20]

"Bring back social union." "Restore the cosmic order." This
language could come straight out of any New Age book. Add this
to Davies' defense of the old pagan practices; add in also the ever-
more-frequent suggestion that we should re-adopt the old pantheon
of gods and goddesses.[21] Does it not suggest that more is brewing
than mere anthropological interest?

Let's think for a minute. Suppose that our society's age-long
disgust for human sacrifice were to change. Suppose further that
some group of people had to be chosen as sacrificial victims to
"bring back social union" and "restore the cosmic order." Who
would be chosen?

Who was chosen for sacrifice in the past? Babies. The handicapped or deformed. The aged. Social dissenters. Religious dissenters.

As this book will show, we are *already* offering human sacrifices from most of these groups. This is the first half of the New Wave. Furthermore, the ground is being prepared to move into sacrificing social and religious dissenters as well. People who don't fit into the New Order. People like Bible-believing Christians.

Confronting the New Age

C. S. Lewis, in one of his famous *Chronicles of Narnia* books, has the boy character looking out his front window in hopes of spying the return of a witch who has escaped from another world. The girl, Polly, says it would be good if the witch never returned, so they wouldn't have to be bothered with her. Digory, the boy, replies, "When there is a wasp in the room, I like to know where it is."

Other writers have exposed the New Agers' theology and their attempts to infiltrate the Christian church. Dave Hunt's *The Seduction of Christianity* and Texe Marrs' *Dark Secrets of the New Age* have laid valuable groundwork. But the question has remained unanswered: exactly *how* would the revolutionary New Agers accomplish their agenda? And how can we stop them?

We believe we have found the answer to that question in the halls of science and government, hospital corridors, and newspaper offices.

The New Age is coming all right . . . not because Christians are unable to fight paganism in our own culture, but because we don't see it.

The wasp is loose.

Let's find it.

PART II:
TO LIVE AND DIE IN THE NEW AGE

FOUR

Come, Sweet Death

Frequently when I'm in a hospital with a "dying"
patient, we are laughing. Out in the hallway, the other
staff members often think we are denying reality. We
must realize that people aren't "living" or "dying," they
are either alive or dead. As long as they are alive, we
must treat them that way. For this reason, I find the
word "terminal" very upsetting. It means we've begun
to treat that person as though he or she were already
dead, incapable of laughter and joy.
(Dr. Bernie Siegel, *Love, Medicine, and Miracles*)

The last enemy to be destroyed is death.
(1 Corinthians 15:26)

The pale young woman slowly got out of the red Ford Escort and reached for her bags. Quickly, scuttling down the steps of the attractive, modern building, a white-uniformed, equally young woman scooped up as much luggage as she could grasp, meanwhile breezily greeting the newcomer. "You're Janice, right? Terminal cancer?"

"Yes, that's right."

"Well, now you won't have to worry about a thing. We'll take care of you."

Janice slowed her pace even more as she approached the steps. "You know, it seems funny, coming here to die. I don't really want to die."

"Ah, this is not the place for that kind of talk!" her new companion retorted. "Here everyone else is beyond the denial stage. They are all learning to accept death as a friend."

41

❦   ❦   ❦   ❦   ❦

Hospice. The word used to mean "a shelter for travelers, children, or the destitute, often maintained by a monastic order."[1] Today it often means "a place where people go to surrender to death without the gospel."

The origins of hospice were in the church. Today, however, much of the movement is secularized, if not downright hostile to Christianity. Some of what the hospice movement has to offer has merit, but many of the workers have something of a ghoulish tinge to their spirit, while others seem to be more motivated by what this work can do for them "as a person" than by serving the patient's life. Too often these volunteers are taught that any spunk on the patient's part, any desire to live, is a form of "denial" which should be discouraged. Patients should refuse to fight off death because Elisabeth Kubler-Ross, the mother of the modern hospice movement, has said, "Death is not an enemy to be conquered."[2] As we have already seen, Scripture says otherwise.

From Kubler-Ross we can discern both the reason why the hospice movement encourages a casual attitude toward death and is hostile toward Christianity and giving the gospel to hospice patients. As she says,

> This work with dying patients has also helped me to find my own religious identity, to know that there is life after death and to know that we will be reborn again one day in order to complete the tasks we have not been able or willing to complete in this lifetime.[3]

Kubler-Ross not only believes in reincarnation but, as a Universalist, believes that *everyone* goes to Heaven (when pinned down to specifics on national television, she said that Adolf Hitler was in Heaven).

Q: On Sunday I was talking to a returned missionary and mentioned to her that I was going to attend a seminar on death and dying. She immediately asked if you were a "Christian" and then went on to elaborate and say the only important thing to know is if the patient was "ready" and knew the "Lord." I knew what she believed but I could only conjure a mental picture of someone running into each patient's room asking if they were "ready to die." How do you break through to these deeply religious people to make them see that there are more facets to dying than the one mentioned above?

A [Kubler-Ross speaking]: I do not regard these people as truly religious, because if they were really such good Christians, they would accept every human being as "thy neighbor" and not judge them as good or bad depending on whether they were Christians or non-Christians . . . [4]

For Kubler-Ross, the passive acceptance of death implanted by Eastern religion is a positive good:

People who have believed in reincarnation, or people from Eastern cultures and religions have often accepted death with unbelievable peace and equanimity even at a young age; whereby many of our Christian patients have had difficulties in their *acceptance of death*.[5]

Why does Kubler-Ross believe in reincarnation? Because of the stories related by some people who claim they have "come back to life" after experiencing medical "death" (which really is not death at all, as we shall see). These people told of going through a tunnel and being welcomed by a glowing being who radiated love and acceptance. After such experiences, the patients typically expressed no fear of death and no feeling of need for the gospel.

Satan, of course, knows how to disguise himself as an "angel of light" (2 Corinthians 11:14). And the Apostle Paul had specifically warned us that if even "an angel from heaven" preached any other gospel than that which requires the blood sacrifice of Jesus Christ as atonement for sin, he should be "accursed" (Galatians 1:8). So Christians will not be taken in by these stories, which explicitly deny not only the gospel but the actual experience of Christians through the ages, who have more often seen unbelievers dying in dreadful fear of Hell than in blissful expectation of Heaven.

Kubler-Ross's New Age view of death, however, is blithely accepted as "scientific" in many quarters.

Now, remember what Nigel Davies, author of *Human Sacrifice in History and Today,* said was necessary to foster an atmosphere in which human sacrifice was considered acceptable:

> The underlying conditions did not alter: lack of any benevolent redeemer, absence of a truly humane ethic, and, finally, belief in a ceaseless cycle of rebirth that turned the death of man into a trivial incident.[6]

"Death That Comes Quickly Is Preferred"

Consider what some medical people are already suggesting about the care of the terminally ill. In response to an article warning of possible ill effects resulting because of the "hospice" approach to death, the following comment appeared in *Mental Retardation,* the journal of a society dedicated to the betterment of the care of mentally retarded people.

> Disparity between the needs of the health care system and human needs sometimes causes the sacrifice of human needs to the larger policy making structure . . .
>
> From a cost/benefit viewpoint, society cannot benefit sufficiently enough from the limited future productivity of such persons to justify spending an increased amount of finite medical resources on them . . .[7]

Dr. Richard Baily, author of *The Dying Patient,* a book published way back in 1970, added this:

> Human life has economic value only as a function of its ability to produce goods and services that are demanded by others. . . .

death that comes quickly is preferred over a lingering terminal illness because direct costs are reduced.[8]

Dr. Wolf Wolfensberger, a professor in the Syracuse University division of Special Education and Rehabilitation, and a tireless worker for the rights of "societally devalued persons," responded to these and similar comments in the August 1984 issue of *Mental Retardation*.

Only time will tell whether this faction within hospice will dominate the hospice movement ...

Imagine accepting a hospice-for-the-dying service, and seeing your (six-month) "deadline" approaching! If you survive it, you feel almost obliged to apologize to all the people who fully expected you to die, and who are now saddled with all sorts of inconveniences and unpleasant obligations by the fact that you are hanging on or—God forbid—even recover ...

Such a service (hospice) also needs to be based on a positive ideology that does not succumb to any of the extremes of death denial, death obsession, or death glorification. [9]

Come, Sweet Death?

Kubler-Ross and her followers so far take a mixed position on promoting death. They vehemently oppose any assisting of people's deaths and any kind of "death pill." Yet, while generally opposing suicide, they will sit a "death-watch" with someone who has taken an overdose so he won't be alone, while doing nothing to save his life. Their acceptance of death seems to be passive rather than active, which as we shall see puts them a notch above the American Medical Association (AMA). Yet, we find disturbing elements about their overall philosophy. Kubler-Ross believes in reincarnation, which in itself makes killing the innocent more acceptable since reincarnationists believe death is just a start on a new life. They also believe in evolution and the New Age concept of "personal growth."

Through commitment to personal growth individual human beings will also make their contribution to the growth and development—the evolution—of the whole species to become all that humankind can and is meant to be.[10]

Since hospicers share terminology and ideology with some of euthanasia's strongest proponents, this does not bode well. Will the hospice remain safe from becoming just another killing center? Government funding for hospices could be used to help convert them into euthanasia centers. It only requires a generation "that knew not Elisabeth Kubler-Ross."

Don't Bury Me

People who work with dying patients report the patient's greatest fear is of being abandoned. The patient instantly recognizes when his loved ones start the slow, agonizing process of distancing themselves emotionally from him. Usually the process begins when he is labeled "terminal." Not that someone should not be told of his true condition, but friends and relatives should not take on a he's-dying-anyway attitude and abandon the friendship they have had at a time like this. This "dying" person is still alive, and more, he is still a *person*, the same person that was there before the word "terminal" entered the picture.

The Christian attitude toward death is well illustrated by a young mother James Dobson featured several times on his radio program, "Focus on the Family." Although Wendy Bergren had painful cancer, from which she eventually died, she refused to consider the alternative of simply surrendering to the cancer and, as she put it, "spending my last days lying on a beach somewhere." Instead, she called her family together and told them that she was going to fight the cancer and try to stay around as wife and mother as long as she possibly could. She was God's servant until the end, making the greatest use of her remaining strength instead of just lolling back in the arms of death.

Arnold Dallimore, in his masterful biography of the great British evangelist George Whitefield, tells of the time Whitefield and a group of ministers were discussing whether a Christian should desire death or not. This was a particularly interesting question for Whitefield, since a great portion of his ministry was performed in great bodily weakness and he had already almost overworked himself to death several times. Some took one position, and some another. Finally they turned to the oldest minister present and asked his opinion. He replied, "I have no opinion about it." When pressed further, he replied irritably, "I said I have no opinion about it! Life and death are God's to decide. How would any of you like to find your servant lying at his ease under a tree, moaning and complaining about the work you have given him and wishing the day were over so he could work no more?"

Christians have two pulls: this life and the next life. Each is good and a gift from God. As the Apostle Paul says,

> For to me, to live is Christ and to die is gain. If I am to go on living in the body, this will mean fruitful labor for me. Yet what shall I choose? I do not know! I am torn between the two: I desire to depart and be with Christ, which is better by far; but it is more necessary for you that I remain in the body. Convinced of this, I know that I will remain ... (Philippians 1:21-25)

We have two pulls, but reincarnationists have only one. The future life, with its step up the scale toward eventual godhood and nirvana, dwarfs the present life. As God says, "All who hate me love death" (Proverbs 8:36).

Love of death may start with accepting it as a "friend." But this new friend is a jealous friend. He demands more and more of those who accept him. As Alexander Pope wrote more than two centuries ago in his famous *Essay on Man,*

> Vice is a creature of such frightful mien
> As to be hated, needs but to be seen.
> Yet seen too oft, familiar with her face
> We first endure, then pity, then embrace.

From enduring death stoically, to having a tender regard for death, to eagerly embracing death are just three steps along a well-greased path that leads, in the end, to *desiring* death for others, as the highest good for them. This then leads to making death *possible,* then *probable,* then *inescapable* for ever more victims.

As we have seen, New Age doctrine teaches that a large number of people need to die to make way for the New Age. We tend to think, when we hear about these grand pronouncements of mass death and destruction, that they are set for far in the future. This is because we have not grasped the mechanism through which this disaster is supposed to occur—through the alliance of paganism and science.

In the next chapters, we will see how the ground has *already* been prepared for this mass sacrifice to the new gods . . . and how the first breaker of the New Wave is already sweeping over its victims.

Cracking the
Weaker Vessels

Human life has economic value only as a function of its ability to produce goods and services that are demanded by others. . . . death that comes quickly is preferred over a lingering terminal illness because direct costs are reduced.

(Richard Baily, *The Dying Patient*)

Whatsoever you do to the least of my brothers, that you do unto me.

(Jesus Christ in Matthew 25:40)

The old woman was sick. Very sick. She could barely swallow. Every mouthful of food and water took a long time to get down.

She was also easily disoriented and feeble.

That was why she was so easy to kill.

First, the nursing home staff did not give her enough time to eat her food. Harassed and underpaid, the woman whose job it was to feed dozens of elderly residents moved through the wards like a robot, shoving food into old people's mouths and yelling, "Eat! Eat!"

The old woman got thinner.

Second, the staff had discovered that an easy way to free up beds for private patients was to move the welfare patients to different rooms. This disoriented them, depressed them, and caused quite a few empty beds.

The old woman was moved.

Surprisingly, she didn't die yet.

She did, however, start to complain about how hungry and unwanted she felt.

It was easy to solve her problems. The doctor prescribed drugs that made her only semiconscious.

Now she did not complain.

She also began to eat even more slowly, when she was able to eat at all.

A feeding tube was inserted.

She developed diarrhea and other complications as a result of the tube. Now she was lying like a pretzel in her lonely bed, unable to move at all.

She got moved again, in spite of her moaning that she wanted to stay where she was.

This time the treatment was successful.

She died.

ぴ   ぴ   ぴ   ぴ   ぴ

Nursing care is not what it used to be in the days of Florence Nightingale. "Inconvenient" people are treated with little or no respect in many cases. As illustrated above, many of our so-called caring institutions abuse people to death, hastening their deaths by surreptitious means. Rather than kill them outright, which might cause legal problems, some methods cause problem patients to die sooner in ways that would not likely be discovered.

Nursing home and hospital patients, particularly the elderly are moved from room to room, floor to floor, upsetting them and making them susceptible to illness. Often they are not given long enough to eat. Those unable to feed themselves may have food-trays plopped in front of them but are not fed. Frequently these people are overmedicated so they will not "complain." Thus already-weak people can easily be made to die.

Dr. Wolf Wolfensberger, an authority on abuses in social services, states,

In many institutional settings, either the physical environment or the service is so poor as to contribute greatly to deaths. For instance, a very common deficiency in nursing homes is not to allow enough time for feeble people to eat. Thus, people become emaciated and prey to death from other causes. It is also known that any discontinuity in the environment of a vulnerable person dramatically increases such a person's vulnerability. Thus, the legitimate-appearing practice of transferring feeble people from one facility to another, one wing to another, one floor to another, one room to another, or even one bed to another, can drastically contribute to disorientation, "senility," stress, depression, etc., and thus to death itself.[1]

Another useful tool for deathmaking is that developed by the sacrifice-minded Aztecs: psychoactive drugs. Wolfensberger goes on to say,

Most informed people in our society are aware that the medical profession has been prescribing psychoactive drugs in excess. However, few people are aware to what extent psychoactive drugs are punitively and destructively administered to societally devalued people. Large proportions of elderly, hyperactive, retarded, mentally disordered, or imprisoned people are on psychoactive drugs, often on several such drugs, and often in large doses. . . . In some institutions and prisons, nearly everyone is on such drugs. These practices have a devastating impact on people's capacity to live, and they contribute to people's death in multiple, often indirect and subtle ways. Since drugs are virtually never listed as causes of death, and since the use of psychoactive drugs is a profoundly disguised way of oppressing devalued people, we can only make an educated guess that such drug uses might contribute to about 100,000 deaths per year—possibly more . . .

In a number of instances, various deadly drugs (e.g., those that paralyze muscles or arrest heart beat) have been systematically and secretly added to patients' intravenous infusions. In a number of hospitals, there have been long strings of such deaths, sometimes over a period of years.

It is my personal estimate that various forms of deathmaking (of which the above are merely a few examples) account for at least 200,000 deaths per year of handicapped and afflicted people. If this estimate is correct, we are killing far more handicapped people per year than the Nazis did between 1939-1945. [2]

Patient-dumping is another way to kill without seeming to kill. An Associated Press story in 1987 informs us that the government has been failing to enforce laws requiring hospitals to treat the poor and uninsured. In response to this laxness, some hospitals have been simply refusing to treat such people at all. Some tactics employed are: refusing to admit the patient, transferring him to another hospital, or making him wait so long that he gives up and leaves. Witnesses at a congressional hearing told of one such instance: a "diabetic neighbor dying after being carried out of the emergency room into the parking lot."[3]

This kind of callousness, and the mistreatment of patients in institutions, would simply be murder if done deliberately, or manslaughter if done through ignorance. But now this kind of maltreatment-to-death is receiving genuine sacrificial status. It is being *justified* as for the *benefit of society*.

Triage in the New Age: Millions for the Machines, None for the People

Triage is "the French military term for the battlefront procedure by which overworked surgeons reject some casualties as too lightly wounded to require treatment, reject others as too badly wounded to be saved, and concentrate their limited resources on the remainder," as a *Time* article on the subject informs us. The article goes on to call triage "a cruel procedure, perhaps an immoral one, but generally regarded as necessary."

Before we go any farther, let's think for a minute about this idea of "limited resources." Some of us remember the scene in *Gone with the Wind* where Scarlett O'Hara finds the doctor among acres of dying and wounded soldiers, with no painkillers and almost no medical supplies with which to help them. Triage was developed for scenes like this, when one man literally did not have the time or supplies to help every wounded soldier. Now think of the tremendous enthusiasm for transplant surgery, which takes enormous amounts of money, supplies, machines, skilled labor, and so on. Transplants are becoming so popular that an *Insight* magazine article lists them as one of three new medical fields that will be responsible for turning around the previously declining need for new doctors. There apparently is *lots* of money for experimental high-tech surgery and the costly medical training and equipment to go with it.

In view of the abandon with which the media are willing to promote $30,000 transplant operations, it certainly is odd that we hear the most about the "need" to limit simple nursing care in order to "conserve limited resources." Feeding elderly patients is "too expensive," whereas experimental operations that each cost enough to provide top-notch nursing care for a year are "vitally necessary to research."

The *Time* article mentioned three criteria for medical triage: by age, by delay, and by money. Again we see the important sacrificial distinction between a privileged class and a devalued class. Supposedly some people are just not worth helping at all. *Time* gave one example:

> Financial triage of various sorts is already taking place even among fully insured patients in the best hospitals. In one New Jersey hospital, for example, there were two thoracic surgeons who did a number of bypass operations. One screened his patients carefully, rejecting smokers, overweight people and other risks; the second accepted sicker patients, including several whom the first had rejected. The second doctor's patients had to stay in the hospital an average of five days longer, and when that showed up on the hospital computers, his privileges were withdrawn on the ground that his work cost the hospital more than insurance carriers were willing to pay . . . [4]

It would seem to make more sense to limit expensive experimental operations and provide decent nursing care for all, if one of the two has to go. High-tech medicine is, after all, the great money-burner, not nursing. High-tech medicine is also of dubious benefit in the majority of cases. When surgeons go on strike, the death rate goes *down!* It would also make more sense to concentrate on developing outpatient and home health care than for insurers (as is common) to only pay for medical work done in a hospital.

But, as we shall see, these sensible solutions cut against the grain of the new pagan medical ethic.

Someone out there *wants* the feeble, the old, the unlovely, the handicapped, and the unprotected to die.

Your Duty to Die: You "Prevent Us from Meeting Other Important Goals"

We have already seen Revolutionary Evolutionary New Age leaders teaching that the "unfit" will not and should not survive the transition to the New Age. Remember what famous Transcendental Meditation teacher Maharishi Mahesh Yogi, declared:

> There has not been and there will not be a place for the unfit. The fit will lead, and if the unfit are not coming along there is no place for them. . . . *Non-existence of the unfit has been the law of nature*. (emphasis ours) [5]

Why the sudden shift in our society from an ethic of compassion for the old, the sick, and the handicapped to an ethic of cost versus benefits? Why this sudden epidemic of abuse and neglect of the medically and socially dependent? Is it just a coincidence that the New Age Movement came out into the open at the same time?

Governor Richard Lamm of Colorado, a state that is a seedbed of the New Age, was one of the first to promote the new ethic, in his famous "Duty to Die" speech. The speech, which gathered much attention and media praise, informed the gathering of old people whom the governor was addressing that it was their duty to die and make way for the young.

CRACKING THE WEAKER VESSELS ☐ 55

The American Hospital Association, for some undiscoverable reason, decided to invite Lamm, now an ex-governor, to address them in 1985. Lamm used the opportunity to lambaste the AHA for what he called "anti-social ethics":

> There are *anti-social ethics* in medicine and health care. Real ethics teach us we must do more than "mean well"; we must also "do good." Medical care is a drain on resources. You are spending America's limited resources. You are trustees of this nation's wealth; you hold part of the future. Health care has the ability to bankrupt America and *to prevent us from meeting other important goals*. You must not look at your specialty, you must survey the whole battlefield. (last emphasis ours)[6]

Lamm continued berating the expenditure of funds on the dying, magnifying their numbers and impact. But he did not stop there; eventually he complained about money being spent on the "chronically ill." This would include diabetics, cystic fibrosis sufferers, and anyone else who frequently requires medical care. Lamm was particularly upset with those who abused their health and indicated that these might not be worthy of any health care at all unless they repented of their ways.

What *are* the "other important goals" that Lamm, and those like him, want us to sacrifice the chronically ill, the overweight, and the elderly to achieve?

"Ye Are Gods: But You Will Die"

Reading and listening to New Agers, one gets the distinct impression that old, sick, and dying people are an offense to them. This is not surprising. Ill and elderly people are the proof positive that we are not gods, that positive thinking does not work, and that reality is not an illusion. God shoots down the New Agers' hope that exalted status among men on earth will give them ultimate control over death in these words:

I said, "You are gods;
you are all sons of the Most High."
But you will die like mere men;
you will fall like every other ruler. (Psalm 82:6, 7)

In the meantime, humanistic scientists, with their concern to divert as much funding as possible to their experimental work, and New Agers, with their gut-level hatred of anything that reminds them of mortality, are jointly declaring that we should cull the "unfit" from society—any way we can. Medical abuse and neglect is only the first sign that this New Wave ethic is beginning to grip.

How far can this New Wave roll?

Where There's a Will

If you are in a coma and on a ventilator and your relatives are not readily available, the odds are that you will be an organ donor.

(Paul A. Byrne and Paul M. Quay,
On Understanding "Brain Death")

Depart from me, you who are cursed, into the eternal fire prepared for the devil and his angels. For I was hungry and you gave me nothing to eat, I was thirsty and you gave me nothing to drink, I was a stranger and you did not invite me in, I needed clothes and you did not clothe me, I was sick . . . and you did not look after me.

(Jesus Christ, speaking of the judgment
of the wicked , Matthew 25:41, 43)

J oe could hear, but he could not talk. The accident had paralyzed him from the neck down, and the shock had made him only partly conscious. Like a dreaming man, there was a fog between him and the world, a feeling of unreality, like being muffled in cotton. So although he knew what was coming when the orderly wheeled him into the operating room, at first he just couldn't follow it.

"All set for a big one?" the team leader asked. "It's a heart transplant, and you know what that means. No slowdowns or foulups. Timing is critical."

Lying there on the table, Joe could hear them talking, but they sounded so far away . . .

Pain. Sharp pain. It sliced through the fog like a knife. The world became clearer. He was being cut . . . They were cutting his chest open!

Wake up, Joe! Say something! Do something!

Joe struggled with the fog—now a blood-red fog, through which white-robed figures danced like ancient priests around the sacrificial altar. He wanted so much to tell them that he was alive, that they should stop cutting him. With a great effort he opened his eyes and looked up at a doctor, scalpel poised in hand, who was just about to start cutting into his tender arteries under the direction of the team leader.

"No," Joe croaked weakly.

"Oh, curse and blast," the doctor fumed. "This one's coming to! Now what are we going to do?"

"Just go ahead," came the cool reply. "The Living Will says if his condition is irreversible—and it is—he's always going to be paralyzed—we don't have to treat him at all, and the Uniform Anatomical Gift Act says we can use his organs if we want to. Nurse, give him a shot of something to make him shut up so we can get on with the operation."

🐦   🐦   🐦   🐦   🐦

Is this a far-fetched story? Science fiction? Not necessarily. As doctor Paul Byrne and legal expert Paul Quay pointed out in their booklet "On Understanding Brain Death,"

The Uniform Anatomical Gift Act was passed in all states in 1970. As a result of this Act, everyone is an organ donor unless there has been "antecedent contrary notice." Permission to take organs is obtained via a descending class of persons going from the person himself or herself, to spouse, to son or daughter, etc., ultimately to any person authorized to dispose of the body, viz, the coroner or the hospital administrator. Thus, if you are in a coma and on a ventilator and your relatives are not readily available, the odds are that you will be an organ donor.[1]

What if you are *not* in a coma or on a ventilator? Are you safe then?

No, thanks to the Living Will laws.

In some states the Living Will legislation is written in such a way that those who have *not* signed one are presumed to have wanted one and are treated as though one existed. Yet there is no way to sign a legal document which would instruct a physician to use every means to save your life! Thus the legislature has granted exclusive control of your medical care to whichever doctor is on duty at the moment.

But What Does It Mean?

Both doctors and the public are being fooled by the language of these so-called "Wills." They appear harmless on their face, but their ambiguous language leaves enough room to drive a carload of scalpels through.

One major promoter of the wills, Concern for Dying, admits, "The determination of exactly when a patient becomes 'terminal' and prognostication of the proximity of death is so medically inexact as to be meaningless."[2]

If nobody can accurately tell when you are "terminal," how could *any* Living Will be worth anything legally? But the real point is that Living Will statutes introduce the idea that refusing to offer basic medical care to patients is OK. In the meantime, some legislation is so strongly worded that a doctor who, for reasons of conscience, cannot comply with the idea of standing by and letting you die is legally liable. So much for all the talk of "choice."

Within the Living Will itself are phrases like "incurable or irreversible condition." Diabetes is an incurable and irreversible condition—but most people who have this disease live fruitful (even if sometimes shorter) lives in spite of it. Yet, according to the letter of the law, if you are diabetic and end up unconscious in a hospital, the doctor on duty could legally refuse to treat you! If this doesn't happen now, it's only because doctors are being *inconsistent,* not because the law *prevents* it.

Another phrase, "any treatment that will only prolong the dying process," is meaningless on its face. The word "treatment" under new guidelines can include *anything* that keeps you alive: food, water, or warmth.

No Living Will legislation requires the hospital to tell you if they are planning to neglect you, and no legislation provides a way to take back the "Do Not Treat" order once treatment (which, remember, includes food, water, and blankets) is being withheld or other provisions have been engaged.

Whose Idea is This, Anyway?
Who dreamed up the Living Will?

It is important to remember that the Living Will was authored by the Society for the Right to Die. The society resulted from the Euthanasia Educational Council, which in turn was created by the Euthanasia Society of America. To quote Dr. Joseph Stanton of Massachusetts: "Fifty-three years ago, in a trial balloon, the Euthanasia Society of America first proposed the direct killing of defective infants at birth.

"Indeed, many people are surprised to learn that in the early decades of this century there was a strong eugenics cult in America...

"In the late 30s and early 40s, the actual killing of over 270,000 hospital patients termed 'useless eaters' in the Third Reich put a quietus on the euthanasia movement."[3]

So the very same group that was pushing for killing babies at birth has now discovered a "compassionate," "sensitive" way to kill medically dependent people at any time. The very same movement that was responsible for the Nazi Holocaust has now emerged as the "respectable" voice of New Wave medical ethics.

Concern for Dying, a main promoter of Living Wills, claims to only favor "passive euthanasia." Yet they are willing to refer people to "active euthanasia" groups like Hemlock, founded by a man (Derek Humphrey) who killed his own wife. Concern's director has even written,

You are right when you say that our people believe rational suicide to be acceptable—our position is that individuals make their own decisions and that those decisions should be honored by others. We also know from experience that if we try to foist our ideas too strongly and too soon on a society not yet ready to consider them, we will damage if not destroy our effectiveness. By moving cautiously and without stridency, we gain a larger audience for our views.

On the subject of crisis centers for potential suicides, or the granting of access to lethal substances, we feel that the time is not yet to take a public position.[4]

"Do Not Help This Person"

The Living Will is not the final word in promoting death instead of medical care. Many patients, young and old, are denied entrance into nursing care institutions unless they will sign a "Do Not Resuscitate" (DNR) order, which is more deadly than a Living Will in that it instructs the staff to make *no effort to save your life* should an emergency arise. A person must sign his or her own death warrant in order to receive care, the extent of which will be for the staff to continue their knitting while they watch you die.

Some institutions simply assign a DNR without any signature. Others go through the formality of a competency hearing, to which the principal is rarely invited, and appoint a "guardian" (who does little guarding) who will sign the DNR.

We recognize that death is not to be fought at *all* costs. It *is* appointed unto man "once to die." Forcibly lengthening the dying process with mechanical life support fails to take into account the Bible's message that pain relief is appropriate for dying people (Proverbs 31:6). The last minutes of life should not ideally be spent hooked to machines and far from family and friends. Having said all that, *forcing* people to sign away their right to emergency care *no matter what* the emergency may be (swallowing a chicken bone the wrong way, for example), is a far cry from respecting an individual's right to a dignified entrance into eternity.

In all these cases, the care-giver simply refuses to give appropriate care, and the patient is not allowed to speak for himself.

These practices are completely at odds with Christian beliefs.

"I Was Sick, and You Pulled My Plug"

Can Christians support the idea of neglecting some people to death, based on prophecies of their future healthiness? Remember Jesus' words:

> When the Son of Man comes in his glory, and all the angels with him, he will sit on his throne in heavenly glory. All the nations will be gathered before him, and he will separate the people one from another as a shepherd separates the sheep from the goats. He will put the sheep on his right and the goats on his left.
>
> Then the King will say to those on his right, "Come, you who are blessed by my Father; take your inheritance, the kingdom prepared for you since the creation of the world. For I was hungry and you gave me something to eat, I was thirsty and you gave me something to drink, I was a stranger and you invited me in, I needed clothes and you clothed me, I was sick and you looked after me . . .
>
> Then the righteous will answer him, "Lord, when did we see you hungry and feed you, or thirsty and give you something to drink? When did we see you a stranger and invite you in, or needing clothes and clothe you? When did we see you sick . . . and go to visit you? [Note: in the Bible, "visit" often means "deliver and bless."]
>
> The King will reply, "I tell you the truth, whatever you did for one of the least of these brothers of mine, you did for me."
>
> Then he will say to those on his left, "Depart from me, you who are cursed, into the fire prepared for the devil and his angels. For I was hungry and you gave me nothing to eat, I was thirsty and you gave me nothing to drink, I was a stranger and you did not invite me in, I needed clothes and you did not clothe me, I was sick . . . and you did not look after me. . . . Whatever you did not do for the least of these, you did not do for me. Then they will go away to eternal punishment, but the righteous to eternal life." (Matthew 25:34ff.)

A Bias in Favor of Death

The Living Will is an obvious tool of the "goats," who in Scripture symbolize Satanists and those deceived by Satan. Living Wills and coercively-obtained, blanket Do Not Resuscitate orders match Jesus' list of the way the "goats" will behave letter for letter. This is a strong prophetic warning to us to stand against such tools of Satan—tools which are bound to be turned on those Jesus calls "the least of these brothers of mine," namely His people.

The New Wave ethic of wiping out the unfit is the real agenda behind Living Wills and Do Not Resuscitate orders. These are *not* pro-choice. There is a *presumption* of death: the victim is presumed to be dying, and this presumption is treated as infallible. The process of causing death by medical action or inaction is *irreversible:* there is no way to say, "Oops, we made a mistake—this patient might live after all!" The process is *impersonal:* the victim is not consulted, and the law presumes you wanted to die. This adds up to a distinct bias in favor of death. All of which is very, very convenient for those who want to rid the earth of the old, sick, and unlovely.

Step Two for the New Wave . . . and more steps are yet to come.

SEVEN

Guardian Angels
of Death

"Medical choices are private, regardless of whether a patient is able to make them personally or must rely on a surrogate," *said the majority opinion [of the New Jersey State Supreme Court].*

(*The Oregonian*, June 26, 1987)

The Arizona Supreme Court has ruled that a person has a right to refuse medical treatment even if the illness is not terminal, and that a guardian may make that choice *if the patient is unable.*

(Associated Press, July 25, 1987)

California already allows dying patients (or their surrogates) *to refuse life-extending treatment,* including food and water.

(San Francisco *Examiner*, October 2, 1987)

A brief, horror-stricken glance at the car lurching drunkenly over the white line into your lane. Screeching tires. The crash of glass. Then ... blackness.

Sirens wail and tires squeal to a stop. You are lifted onto a stretcher. Passersby slow down to watch as you are carefully carried into the ambulance.

In the emergency room, everything is ready to receive you. The blood from the last accident victim has been cleared away.

Scrubbed nurses bustle about, setting out instruments.

As they lay you on the table, the head doctor looks down at you. "Hmm. Bad damage to the head, but looks healthy otherwise. Tell you what. I think we can use this one. Put him on a respirator while we check it out."

Quickly secretaries go through your identification and call your relatives. Nobody's home. Meanwhile, interns work on you to stop the bleeding and nurses hook you up to machines.

The head doctor gets the report that your relatives are unavailable. He smiles. "That's all right. We'll just assume legal guardianship."

You are wheeled into the operating room. There they cut you open, remove your organs, and wheel you out . . . dead.

❦   ❦   ❦   ❦   ❦

Surely this *is* a New Age in medical care—where a third party can doom you to a lingering death and claim he or she is acting as your "guardian." The language of the Guardian Acts and Living Will laws calls these people "surrogate decision-makers," implying that they are just doing for you what you would naturally want to do for yourself. After all, don't we *all* want to die of hunger and thirst? Don't we all want to become involuntary organ banks, to have simple medical care denied, and so on?

In California your "surrogate" can order the hospital to refuse you food and drink.

In Arizona your "guardian" can prevent you from receiving any medical care, including food and water, even if you are *not* diagnosed as "terminal." You only have to be "incompetent," and all *that* means is that the judge is willing to give control over you to someone else who can make it to the courtroom.

In New Jersey, your relatives can collect huge sums for malpractice if a doctor's mistake puts you into a coma—and then order you put to death by starvation and thirst. They are exercising *your* "right to privacy" when they do this, according to the New Jersey Supreme Court.

In Oregon, Senate Bill SB20 attempted to allow fifteen-year-olds to sign a legal document giving their family the right to withhold "nutritional fluids" from them, should some doctor label them "terminally ill."[1]

Washington state legislators recently tried to attach an amendment to the existing Living Will law that "would make starvation and dehydration of patients legal *even when they had not signed Living Wills.*" This bill, which died in committee, would have made it "legal to withhold spoon-feeding from Altzheimer's patients."[2]

Daniel Callahan, director of the Hastings Ethics Center, the most prestigious organization today in the area of "bio-ethics," has said in support of such laws, "A denial of nutrition [meaning starving people to death] may in the long run become the only effective way to make certain that a large number of biologically tenacious [he means they are alive and threatening to stay that way] patients actually die." Callahan was well aware of the implications of giving third parties the authority to kill at will:

"Given the increasingly large pool of superannuated, chronically ill, physically marginal elderly," Callahan continued, "it could well become the nontreatment of choice. Second, because we have now become sufficiently habituated to the idea of turning off the respirator, we are psychologically prepared to go one step further."[3]

Just Trust Me, I'm Your Guardian Angel

Guardianship, right now, is mainly used to deprive elderly people of all their civil rights.

The 300,000 to 400,000 elderly people under guardianship can no longer receive money or pay their bills. They cannot marry or divorce. The court entrusts to someone else the power to choose where they will live, what medical treatment they will get and, in rare cases, when they will die. . . .

Elderly persons in guardianship court are often afforded fewer rights than criminal defendants. In 44 percent of the cases, the proposed ward was not represented by an attorney. Three out of ten files contained no medical evidence. Forty-nine percent of the wards were not present at their hearings. Twenty-five percent of the files contained no indication hearings had been held.

Some elderly people discover that they are wards of the court only after the fact. . . .

If granted, guardianship reduces the "wards of the court" to the status of legal infants who may no longer drive a car, vote or, in many states, hire an attorney.

"A prisoner has more legal rights," said Winsor Schmidt, a Memphis State University professor who has studied guardianship in 13 states.

Once shuffled into guardianship, the elderly have few ways out. Some states bar wards from hiring attorneys because they have been ruled incompetent. . . . [4]

Originally designed as a way of protecting elderly people from harming themselves (i.e., from handing all their savings over to swindlers), guardianship is increasingly invoked as a way to deprive the elderly of their *medical* rights—that is, their right to choose or reject treatments and to pick their own medical care providers.

"Guardianship is a process that uproots people, literally 'unpersons' them, declares them legally dead," said Dr. Dennis Koson, a law and psychiatry expert in Florida. "Done badly, it does more hurting than protecting."

That danger was confirmed by the investigation, which involved staff reporters in every state. . . .

The Associated Press found institutions are increasingly using guardianship as an answer to a variety of problems. Hospitals, faced with new Medicare regulations limiting coverage for extended care, use guardianship to move patients to nursing homes. Nursing homes now require guardianship to ensure someone will pay the bills. . . .

Nursing homes, hospitals and doctors also are using guardianship as a hedge against liability in tough decisions such as amputation and disconnecting life-support systems. . . . [5]

How interesting. According to this Associated Press report, the "rights" being protected are actually the rights of medical people who want to make decisions without consulting, or against the will of, their patients.

Guardianship, in other words, makes these old people literally into the *slaves* of their guardians. The "guarded" elderly can't even hire attorneys to protest their treatment!

Considering that guardianship is such a major denial of basic constitutional rights, surely judges are extremely careful about granting guardianship, right?

Wrong. As the report continues,

> When held, guardianship hearings sometimes last only minutes. Medical investigators and court-appointed examiners often perform perfunctory checks of proposed wards to see if guardianship is needed.
>
> Competency examinations, when they are done, are performed by people with varying degrees of expertise, including urologists, osteopaths, social workers, nursing home employees and retired court clerks. Their decisions may be based on such tests as the proposed ward's ability to recall the names of the last three presidents or perform simple math problems.
>
> Whatever the criteria, and whoever is making the judgment, in 94 percent of the cases examined by the Associated Press the petition for guardianship was approved. . . .[6]
>
> Naming a guardian or conservator is frequently a paper process, lacking many of the due process provisions afforded someone being committed to a mental institution, such as a court hearing or a lawyer for the proposed ward. . . .
>
> The AP surveyed 62 guardianship and conservatorship case files on elderly people dating from 1979 to the present in seven of Oregon's 36 counties. The AP found:
>
> • Guardianships and conservatorships are rarely turned down. The survey showed 97 percent of the petitions were approved.
>
> • Wards rarely have the benefit of counsel. None of the wards in the survey was represented by a lawyer, unless the ward initiated the case.

> • It doesn't take much evidence to convince a judge. Only 42 percent of the wards were examined by a doctor before being declared incompetent. . . .[7]

This is what it means to have a "guardian" or "surrogate" make medical decisions "in your best interest." Any relative, medical person, or government official who has the time and money to convince a judge in your absence that you are "incompetent" (which you obviously are, since you couldn't hop out of your hospital bed to get to the courtroom) can abuse you to death *legally.* The media will then uphold his actions as "compassionate," since you certainly would have *wanted* to be abused to death if anyone had chosen to consult you. Which they will not bother to do. Furthermore, if you object to the way you are being treated, it does not matter at all, since once you have a "guardian" you have *no legal right to be heard.* When you cry, "Water, water!" and the order on your case says, "No liquids," the nurses would be *breaking the law* to bring you water.

New Age Nazis

What most of us don't realize is that these "guardian" acts are the sign that our medical and legal establishments *no longer reject the Nazi way of doing things.* All the arguments for allowing third parties to doom victims to death were already tried and found wanting—at the famous Nuremburg war crimes trials.

> At the Nuremburg war crimes trials in 1945 and '46, the doctors who had participated in the atrocities defended their research by saying that the prisoners were doomed anyway. As one physician who dissected prisoners' brains put it, "I accepted those brains, of course; where they came from and how they came to me was really none of my business."
>
> Such an argument implies that inmates on the verge of death forfeit rights that the hale and hearty and free take for granted. The Nuremburg panel rejected this position, and the evidence of grossly brutal research introduced at that trial spawned the

Nuremburg code, which established minimum standards for what may be done to humans for experimental purposes. The central position of the code holds that "the voluntary consent of the human subject is absolutely essential. . . . The duty and responsibility for ascertaining the quality of the consent rests upon each individual who initiates . . . the experiments." Other cases have further refined the doctor's ethical responsibility. The outcry that followed the disclosure in 1972 of the Tuskeegee experiment, in which U.S. Public Health Service left 600 impoverished black men with syphilis untreated for 40 years in order to study the course of the disease, reinforced the tenet that a doctor may not withhold care for scientific reasons. The backlash from that experiment expanded the researcher's responsibility, to include the principle that an experimental procedure must offer the subject some chance of medical benefit. . . . [8]

The Nuremburg panel stressed that "voluntary consent" must rule in medical care, and that "an experimental procedure must offer the subject some chance of medical benefit." Surely they meant this to apply to *non*-experimental procedures as well. After all, we *know* that if we give a sick old lady nothing to eat or drink, she will die, and that this "procedure" offers her *no* "chance of medical benefit."

Now is as good a time as any to make it clear that the Nazi agenda, which Nuremburg rejected and our modern medical establishment has now embraced, was a *New Age agenda*. Texe Marrs tells us in his best-seller *Dark Secrets of the New Age,*

Hitler's poisonous racial theories were not far afield from those of the New Age extremists. The Aryan race was to become the man-god race of a thousand-year Reich founded by Hitler and his monstrous SS troops. It is no coincidence that, like those of New Age leaders today, Hitler's theories were grounded in the occult and in the teachings of Theosophy and Hinduism. Furthermore . . . Hitler, too, believed in the masters of Shamballa and in the superiority of a Tibetan occultism. . . .

The Fuhrer supposed that he was to be the New Age Christ

and . . . inaugurate the world into its new higher state of consciousness. [9]

A book Texe Marrs quotes, intriguingly titled *New Age Bible Interpretation,* tells us that "Seven Root Races succeed one another in the racial evolution on a planet during a world Period . . . Aryan [is] the term applied to the Fifth root race."[10]

Marrs also quotes another book, *The Twisted Cross,* by Joseph J. Carr. This book demonstrates that

The Nazis worshiped pagan gods, that the dreaded SS (Gestapo) conducted Mystery initiation rites and swore blood oaths to Satan, and that the top Nazi leaders were dedicated students of the black magic arts and witchcraft. The Nazis also believed in evolution, karma, and reincarnation—all New Age concepts.

Hitler himself was an avid reader of occult literature and a member of the occultist Thule Society. The swastika, the Nazi symbol of a twisted cross, is itself an occult religious symbol found frequently in ancient times on the altars of pagan gods and still seen today on the walls of some Hindu temples in India. . . .[11]

Carr tells us that Dietrich Eckart, a Master Adept of the Thule Society, told others in the Society that his demon spirit master had revealed to him that he was chosen to "train up a 'vessel for the Antichrist' who would lead the Aryan race to great triumph and victory over the Jews."

The chosen vessel for Eckart's ministrations was Adolf Hitler. Eckart urged his disciples to support Hitler, crowing,

He [Hitler] will dance but it is I who will call the tune! I have initiated him into the SECRET DOCTRINE, opened his centers of vision and given him the means to communicate with the powers.[12]

Why is it that our own leaders are now supporting the Nazi way of doing things? Why have they rejected the perfectly good ethics laid out at Nuremburg in favor of promiscuous killing of medically dependent people? Why are we hearing the exact same arguments the Nazis put forth—about "wasting resources" and so on—without any exposure of their Nazi origin? Why, after pro-lifers have spent more than a decade carefully pointing out the connection between abortion and the Nazi Holocaust, has the mere mention of the term "Nazi" become a signal to the media to *ignore* what is being said?

What will happen when third parties take over as primary decision-makers in medical matters?

What is happening *now?*

Something wicked this way comes . . .

Of course, it would be even more of a coup for Satan if people would just learn to ritually kill themselves off, as they so often did in pagan cultures. Then guardians wouldn't even be needed to ensure a constant stream of sacrifices to the New Age gods of beauty, money, sex, and power.

This part of the Plan, too, is underway . . .

EIGHT

Dance to the Devil

Both students planned their suicides quite carefully.
They left instructions for their funerals and chose their
own pallbearers. Rodman wanted to be buried in his
football jersey and laid out in state in the school gymna-
sium. Darcine had requested that the football team be
her pallbearers. She had her cabbage patch doll in her
coffin.

> *Does this sound like "low self-image" to you? It*
sounds more like the manifestations of a death cult.
> (Samuel Blumenfeld, writing in
> *The Blumenfeld Education Letter)*

In the 1980's the subject of death and dying will become
an accepted and essential aspect of the health education
curriculum.

> (The National Education Association,
> *Education in the 80's)*

All who hate me love death.

> (God, quoted in Proverbs 8:26)

S andy trembled and shook in her chair, moaning,
screaming, struggling against some unseen
assailant.

"Let me go!" she screamed. "Let me go!"

Her eyes were wide open, but she was seeing unspeakable
horrors from another world. She gasped for air, pale with terror.

She's going to die, Brummel! They are going to kill her!

The hulking, bug-eyed creature sitting in Langstrat's chair

73

was bellowing in a voice that made Brummel's insides quiver. "You are lost, Sandy Hogan! We have you now! You belong to us, and we are the only reality you know!"

"Please, God," she screamed. "Get me out of here, please!"

"Join us! Your mother has fled, your father is dead! He is gone! Think of him no longer! You belong to us!"

Sandy went limp in her chair as if she had been shot, her face suddenly numbed with despair. . .

"Kill the girl!" Rafar shouted to Madeline.

Madeline drew out a horrible crooked knife. She placed it gently in Sandy's hand. "These chains are the chains of life; they are a prison of evil, of the lying mind, of illusion! Free your true self! Join me!"

Shawn had a knife ready. He placed it in the entranced Sandy's hand.

❦   ❦   ❦   ❦   ❦

The scene above, from Frank Peretti's gripping novel *This Present Darkness* (Crossway Books, 1986), shows a young girl whom demons are trying to deceive into killing herself. Meanwhile, a real live human being named Shawn is hovering nearby, ready to give her the physical knife with which she will do the job.

Truth is sometimes more bizarre than fiction. Today the National Education Association, pro-suicide groups, and rock musicians are banding together to promote death for teens—death leading to either simple nonexistence or an eternity in the arms of Satan, depending on whether the "respectable" NEA and suicide groups or the more honest rock musicians are doing the talking.

As noted education author Samuel Blumenfeld warned in his *Blumenfeld Education Letter* of February 1987,

> Something is being put into the minds of young people persuading them that death is preferable to life.
> According to the *NEA Journal* of November 1964, 550 teenagers killed themselves in 1962. Why are ten times as many

killing themselves today? Obviously, two thoughts or feelings must be in a person's mind or heart before that person commits suicide: life must be viewed as unbearable, unlivable, and therefore hated; and death must be viewed as a preferred, if not pleasant, alternative. To simplify it all: a person who hates life and loves death is much more likely to commit suicide than one who loves life and hates death.

Are American public schools teaching children to hate life and love death? The answer is a resounding yes. How is this done? Through lessons in values clarification, which teach hatred of life, and lessons in death education, which teach love of death.

Learning to Hate Life Through Values Elimination

As Mr. Blumenfeld goes on to explain, values clarification classes force children to make life-and-death decisions on the basis of pagan ethics—choosing *whom* to put to death out of a hypothetical group. This group often includes close family members, as in the Nuclear War exercise, where children have to choose *which* parent to send out to die from nuclear radiation, since the hypothesized radiation shelter can only handle one adult and one child (them). The Lifeboat Game is also popular. In this "game," children are asked to imagine a lifeboat fully stocked with stereotypical characters: an old clergyman, a country-western singer, a young black activist, and so on. One of these people must be tossed overboard to the sharks, and it is up to the children to decide which. Professor Richard Mitchell points out:

This is *not* one of the contexts in which the educationists choose to warble paeans to "the uniqueness and absolute worth of the individual." . . . In this case, the verdict must be "relevant," conducive to "the greatest good for the greatest number," and the exclusive focus on accepted notions of "social usefulness" assures that *a* decision *will* be made. Another *kind* of inquiry—whether it is better to *do* or *suffer* an injustice, for instance, or whether the *common good* is more to be prized than the *good*—would preclude decision and spoil the game . . .What a pity that Himmler and Goebbels and all that crowd are dead.

They'd make really neat resource persons for the Lifeboat
Game.[1]

The students are also taught that "there is no God, that they
are animals without souls, the products of evolution, and that all
they have to look forward to is a nuclear holocaust."[2] Not surprisingly, some reject this vision of their futures—and their own lives
with it.

Learning to Love Death through Suicide Education

But, as Mr. Blumenfeld mentioned, values clarification is only half
of the schools' equation. The other half is the new specialty of
death education.

> Death education removes the fear and mystery of death and
> makes suicide more palatable. In death education children visit
> cemeteries and funeral homes. They may try out the coffins or
> watch the mortician embalm a corpse. They plan their own funer-
> als, write their own obituaries, discuss suicide at great length:
> how to do it, when to do it, why to do it. They even write suicide
> notes. And of course they discuss euthanasia. (Blumenfeld, op.
> cit.)

It certainly seems more than a bit odd that, supposedly in
response to the growing problem of teen suicide, the NEA is
teaching children *how* and *why* to commit suicide. This led Mr.
Blumenfeld to ask a startling question:

> Are "death educators" normal human beings or are they the pur-
> veyors of a satanic death cult that has taken hold of the schools?
>   The only "death educator" I've met is the one I interviewed
> at a high school in Massachusetts where they've had an unusually
> high incidence of suicide. He was a tall, slim man in his late thir-
> ties or early forties who taught "health education." . . .

I asked him if he expected the situation to improve or get worse at his school. He asked me what I meant by improvement. I said I meant a decrease or an end to the suicides. His reply was quite unexpected. "It's a matter of opinion whether that would be an improvement or not," he said.

In view of this attitude, increasingly widespread among death ed instructors in the government schools, the *way* teens are committing suicide can lead to more questions. For example, the fifteen-year-old Michigan boy accused of shooting his older brother to death did it on February 2, a witches' sabbath. While investigating the murder, the police found, among other things, "inverted crucifix medallions, books on satanic ritual, a dagger, a black-hooded robe, and tape recordings of heavy metal rock music."[3]

Note that the schoolchildren are also led into discussions of euthanasia while they are being desensitized to suicide. This is probably no coincidence. For, at the very same time, forces are at work trying to change the laws to "allow" doctor-administered death to anyone, including a child, who momentarily despairs of life.

New Age Death in California

The hotspot for pro-suicide legislation is, predictably, California, the original home of the New Age Movement.

LOS ANGELES (AP) California Bar Association delegates have approved a resolution supporting "doctor-assisted suicide," which would allow physicians to give terminally ill patients a prescription for a lethal dose of drugs.

After an intense debate, delegates to the group's annual meeting voted 282-239 on Sunday to direct the organization's Board of Governors to back a euthanasia bill before the Legislature.[4]

California voters will be the first in the world to decide on such a law [Humane and Dignified Death Act], according to the World

Voluntary Euthanasia Conference. Active voluntary euthanasia is legal in Holland, but it came about by supreme court decision, not by popular vote.

California already allows dying patients (or their surrogates) to refuse life-extending treatment, including food and water. But this *passive* euthanasia, or "allowing to die," is a far different act than the proposed *active* euthanasia. . . .

It would require a fundamental change in the law, but it's a change we may be ready to make. . . . [5]

Suffer, Little Children

No sooner was the ink dry on the proposed suicide legislation than the media was giving attention to people who want to use this legislation to encourage teen suicide. An article in the Washington *Times,* for example, entitled "Pro-Suicide Activists Call for Right to Assist," featured this call for teen sacrifice:

Margaret P. Battin, associate professor of philosophy at the University of Utah at Salt Lake City, said yesterday that even teenagers—at least those with catastrophic illnesses or severe mental impairments— should be entitled to receive help in killing themselves if they believe death would be beneficial. . . .

The conference was sparked by efforts of the Hemlock Society, a think tank for the euthanasia movement, to get a law on the books in California that would allow terminally ill patients— expected to live no more than six months—to ask their physicians for lethal injections or drug overdoses to end their suffering. . . .

Although the California proposal would not legalize suicide assistance for elderly persons unless they were dying, Nancy Osgood, assistant professor of gerontology at the Medical College of Virginia in Richmond, said she foresees the possibility of older people killing themselves in response to such legislation. She said she also sees the prospect of terminally ill patients who may not be interested in accelerating their deaths nevertheless doing so because of the new law. *"When something becomes acceptable, it can almost become obligatory,"* Ms. Osgood said. "If suicide becomes acceptable, it could create a climate of opinion in which older people and those terminally ill start killing themselves because *they believe that is what people want."* (Emphasis ours)[6]

No Parental Consent Needed

We have seen what the "no parental notification" laws have done for teen abortion. Now such laws are being proposed for child suicide.

A proposal has been submitted in the Netherlands to allow children under the age of 16 to request physician-assisted suicide without parental consent.[7]

Read that again. Children *under* the age of 16 in the Netherlands would be "allowed" to "request" their own murder at the hands of a doctor. The parents would not even be able to determine whether this was the child's *own* request or if the child had been brainwashed, coerced, or forced into requesting suicide—since the child would be dead before the parents even knew what happened.

The picture begins to get a little clearer.

(1) The National Education Association, an organization notorious for its hostility to Christianity and Christian values, is using values clarification to systematically attack children's belief in God and His laws.

(2) The NEA is also using death education as a vehicle for promoting suicide.

(3) "Pro-suicide activists" want doctors to be able to murder children without the parents' knowledge—supposedly at the child's own request, but with no way for the parents to check up on this.

Substitute "Satanists" for doctors and black hooded robes for the white coats, and this would be the perfect prescription for an unparalleled revival of child sacrifice, equalling the abortion holocaust in scope. It would also be a tremendous way to get a constant supply of young, healthy organs, which as we shall see would be a strong motivation to today's medical establishment to promote this sort of "suicide."

The best part, as far as Satan is concerned, is that all these children would go into eternity without any chance to hear the gospel, repent, and get saved. Although even condemned murderers in America have always been given lengthy opportunities to have chaplains preach to them, suicide cases would be *insulated* from even their parents' desperate attempts at sharing the truth. And since according to the new pagan ethic of government, we must "separate church and state," it would probably be considered "establishing a religion," not to mention interfering with the victim's "right to privacy," for a Christian clergyman to visit the potential suicide and try to share the gospel and why suicide is wrong. For it would be our *government,* through the person of state-approved doctors, who would be doing the killing.

Human sacrifice: "The murder, torture, and/or cannibalism of an innocent person justified as beneficial for himself, for another person, or for society." State-administered death to those supposedly requesting suicide: "The murder of an innocent person justified as beneficial for himself or (in the case of those with 'catastrophic illnesses' or 'severe mental impairments' whom pro-death activist Margaret Battin mentioned) for society."

And Mother Kali, the Hindu death goddess, wears a necklace of *children's* skulls . . .

NINE

Euphemasia

West German teenagers asked in the schools during the 1980s what they knew about Hitler often noted that he wasn't all bad as a person or for society, because after all, he arranged for merciful deaths for handicapped people.

(Dr. Wolf Wolfensberger)[1]

If the god was to be duly honoured, his living image had to die with dignity.

(Nigel Davies, *Human Sacrifice in History and Today*)[2]

The young woman had been in a terrible car crash. Her pelvis broke, killing her unborn child. But the tragedy was not over yet. An anesthetic disaster occurred while removing her dead infant and she was left severely brain damaged.

She was placed in a nursing home and lived there only requiring a feeding tube because she could not swallow. She was active, responsive to commands; she could see and hear and feel pain and was aware of her surroundings.

Her care was completely covered by insurance.

After seven years, long enough for her husband to collect the $900,000 award as a settlement of the suit on her behalf, he sought to have the feeding tube removed. The case went to the New Jersey State Supreme Court, which finally ruled in the husband's favor. Thus, Nancy Ellen Jobes died of starvation and thirst on August 7, 1987.

The media, uncomfortable with the facts, called her "comatose" and "unconscious," but she was neither. New Jersey has come a long way from removing a respirator from Karen Ann Quinlan, who *was* comatose and totally unresponsive, to killing the merely inconvenient Nancy Ellen Jobes. Her murder was one of the first open sacrifices to a new medical ethic.

In Memory of Nancy

Let us look a little more closely at what happened to Nancy Ellen Jobes, and why she was condemned to that slow, painful death. Here are two reports on the Jobes case, each of which presents facts suppressed by the major media, and each of which casts new light on what exactly happened in that New Jersey courtroom.

First, Dr. Wolf Wolfensberger's report. This man, who survived the Nazi Holocaust and who has spent years of his life observing and fighting the deteriorating medical and social service situation in the USA, had this to say about the Jobes case.

> It involved a 32-year old woman who became profoundly debilitated as a result of an error or accident in the administration of anesthesia during surgery when she was 25. Her family waited until their lawsuit for damages was settled in their favor for $900,000—and then requested withholding of food and water, describing her as an ugly not human monstrosity who died a long time ago and should have a funeral now, who was not living and not a human entity. The court dismissed the testimony of the nursing home employees who worked with the woman every day as illusions, and accepted as credible the testimony that described the women as ugly, monstrous, and inhuman.[3]

Writing in *World* magazine, pro-life advocate Rita Marker also got to the heart of the matter with her pungent report:

On June 24, the New Jersey Supreme Court added a new offense to the list of crimes for which a person can be sentenced to death:

Being brain-damaged and too healthy to die. . . .

Jobes' family, described in news accounts as caring and suffering, postponed the request to stop Jobes' food and fluids until after a $900,000 settlement had been made in the malpractice suit against the anesthesiologist at the hospital where her injuries occurred. . . .

The question was not "Could she live?" but rather, "Should she live?"

Those opposing her right to continued food and fluids described her as "ugly," "a monstrosity," and "not human." Neurologist David Carlin said, "She died a long time ago . . . She should have a funeral." Another neurologist, Henry Liss, said, "She's not living, she's not a human entity."

Lincoln Park Nursing Home, where Jobes has been a patient for six years, strongly opposed the request. Home officials observed, "She is not terminally ill . . . She responds to touch and sound stimuli . . . follows movements of a person with her eyes . . . reacts to pain . . . There is no competent evidence that Nancy would want to terminate her life."

Two neurologists, Maurice Victor, coauthor of a leading neurology textbook, and Allan Ropper, associate professor at Harvard Medical School, testified about her awareness and responsiveness. Ropper reported: Jobes can see and hear; she responds to commands; her movements are purposeful and volitional; she fatigues and can feel pain. . . .

Jobes' husband, who according to court records did not visit her for a year, may now preside over her death—a lingering, painful death that could take from six to 15 days. Such a death, if imposed for any other "criminal" offense, would most assuredly be deemed "cruel and unusual punishment."[4]

So here we have a "warm" and "caring" husband who does not even bother to visit his wife for a year . . . who holds up his request for her slow death by starvation long enough to collect almost a million dollars from a malpractice suit, and then refuses to spend any of the sum granted on the further care of his wife . . . and who introduces courtroom witnesses who call his wife a "monster" and "not a human entity." Here we also have a judge who disregards the testimony of neurologists about Nancy Jobes' *actual physical capacities* and the testimony of nursing home workers who have observed her every day, and instead accepts emotional, unscientific labels based on some other neurologists' personal reaction to Nancy Jobes' *appearance*. The judge further had the gall to order the nursing home to starve and thirst torture Jobes to death, despite the conscientious objections of the nursing home workers to this kind of death-dealing. Perhaps sensing the bad press he would get if he had to send in police to force the nursing home workers to torture Nancy to death, he did cave in at the last minute and have Nancy transferred to a hospital where the staff had no objections to presiding over the death by slow torture of a helpless woman who was able to sense her environment and feel and respond to pain.

Court 1, Conroy 0

Nancy Jobes is not the only victim of the New Jersey courts. Claire Conroy also came within an inch of being sacrificed by the court, just because someone wanted her out of the way. She was not comatose or vegetative and she was able to respond to some commands, move in accordance with her own wishes, feel and hear. Yet the judge, ruling that Claire could be starved to death, demeaned the doctors' and nurses' testimonies regarding Conroy's abilities, accusing them of being (as if it were a crime) pro-life. He ruled that her life had become intolerably and permanently burdensome.

But burdensome to whom? Did he read her mind?

Evidently the New Jersey Supreme Court believes that someone read Claire's mind, because they concluded, "The right of an adult who, like Claire Conroy, was once competent, to determine the course of her medical treatment remains intact *even when she is no longer able to assert that right or to appreciate its effectuation*" (emphasis ours).

In other words, she has the right to die painfully even if someone else does the deciding for her.

A dangerous thing, being incommunicado.

The entire case was riddled with loaded terminology like "intolerably and permanently burdensome," "proxy," "surrogate decision maker," "nutrition and hydration," and "competence." The mainstream press, acting more as Madison Avenue pitchmen for New Wave medical ethics than in the media's historic role as critic, faithfully used all these terms in its coverage, thus distracting most people from the real issue in the Conroy case.

Miss Conroy had no fatal disease. She was not dying—in fact, that was the "problem." So the court ruled that others could *cause her death* through induced starvation and thirst. The judge did not dare to say, "Go ahead and kill her." Instead, the whole procedure was renamed "allowing her to die."

One brave judge in the appellate court recognized the truth, writing, "The trial judge authorized euthanasia [homicide]. . . . " He was overturned.

Conroy finally beat her assailants by dying of other causes before they could starve her. Unfortunately, the court's decision lives.

Kill the "Pleasantly Senile"

In an article in *America* magazine in 1987, writer Richard A. McCormick points out the significant difference between the *Conroy* case and the previous landmark *Herbert* euthanasia case:

> These two cases have a key difference. Clarence Herbert was judged to be in a permanent vegetative state. Claire Conroy was not . . .
>
> Even more recently a group of distinguished clinicians advocated the withholding of parenteral fluids and nutritional support from severely and irrevocably demented patients and, occasionally, from elderly patients with permanent mild impairment of competence, a group characterized as "pleasantly senile" (*New England Journal of Medicine,* 1984) . . .
>
> This suggests the wisdom of Daniel Callahan's statement at a spring conference on these problems in 1984: "The time to curtail abuses in the future is to begin now in trying to go through those steps that will draw lines very carefully." We have moved from Quinlan (persistent vegetative state—removal of respirator) to Herbert (persistent vegetative state—removal of respirator, naso-

gastric tube and I.V. lines) to Conroy (incompetent but noncomatose—removal of nasogastric tube). The progression is obvious, and obviously dangerous, unless we draw clear lines based on clear criteria. If we do not, we will not long be confined within the limits set forth in cases like Conroy.[5]

The Men in the Black Robes

The cases of Nancy Jobes and Claire Conroy are significantly parallel to one of the Aztecs' more unusual sacrifical rituals. Modern anthropologists call it the Gladiatorial Sacrifice. It started with trumpets and conch shells sounding, to give an air of importance to what was about to follow. Then the first of the preselected victims was given a ceremonial drink and made to climb up on the round sacrificial stone. Following is a description of the Gladiatorial Sacrifice, taken down by a Spanish priest, Fray Bernardino de Sahugun, in the words of the Aztec believers themselves.

> Then the wolf-priest took the rope holding the captive, which reached and was attached to the centre of the stone; then he tied it about the waist of the captive. And he gave him a war club, decked with feathers and not set with obsidian blades. And he placed before him four pine cudgels, his missile, with which to lay about him, with which to defend himself. [6]

The victim then had to fight off, with his club set only with feathers, four opponents who had weapons of flint. Even if he managed this incredible feat, he was doomed nonetheless, for the fifth and final opponent always delivered a stroke that could not be parried forehand. The blood was then poured through the hollow cane decked with feathers onto the lips of the stone idols, while the body was flayed and eaten. Only the man who had originally captured the victim in battle ate none, "for when he first won the prisoner on the battlefied, he uttered the traditional words, 'He is as my beloved son.'"[7]

The symbolism of the Aztec rite is obvious. The victim was given a chance to defend himself—but it was a mock chance. His end was predetermined from the beginning of the unequal contest. Finally the very man who had handed him over to a horrible death showed his "compassion" for the victim by refusing to join in the cannibal feast that followed.

The priests, dignified in their robes and preceded with ceremonial sounding of trumpets, presided over the whole event, not to make sure the victim got a fair chance, but to make sure he did not.

We can learn something from this about the New Wave and how the New Age agenda can be enforced in our society. Just as under the Aztecs, the victim will be given an illusion of rights and a fair trial. Yet none of the logical testimony entered on behalf of the person slated for death will be given any more weight than it was given in the *Jobes* and *Conroy* cases. Any more weight than . . . feathers.

Death Without Dignity

The term *euthanasia* used to mean dying when you were mentally prepared for it: dying well and gracefully. After all, its literal meaning is "good death." Under present use, euthanasia is just killing—often extremely painful killing. Its advocates call it "good death," because the victim is sacrificed for a "good" purpose. His death, however, is not really "good" in the moral sense but rather "good for" someone else.

Remember the definition of human sacrifice from Chapter 2?

"The murder, torture, and/or cannibalism of an innocent person justified as beneficial for himself, for another person, or for society."

According to this definition, which is based on the actual mind-set and practice of pagan tribes, *Nancy Ellen Jobes and Claire Conroy were human sacrifices.* Sacrificed to the god of Mammon for the family's and society's economic benefit. Sacrificed to appease the Venus cult—a judge, neurologists, and journalists who find physically unlovely people disgusting. Sacrificed just like the worst of the pagan sacrifices—with a long, lingering, painful death.

What Is It Like to Die of Hunger and Thirst?

If we want to minister to the humanity of the people who are so vulnerable—the dying, the brain damaged and the comatose—we would do well to find out exactly what happens to people when doctors "pull the plug." In one case, trial judge David Kopelman sought a list of effects to a person starving and dehydrating due to the apparently casual "removal of nutrition and hydration."

This is what the judge found out:

(a) His mouth would dry out and become caked with or coated with thick material.

(b) His lips would become parched or cracked or fissured.

(c) His tongue would become swollen and might crack.

(d) His eyes would sink back into their orbits.

(e) His cheeks would become hollow.

(f) The mucous (lining) of his nose might crack and cause his nose to bleed.

(g) His skin would hang loose on his body and become dry and scaly.

(h) His urine would become highly concentrated, causing burning of the bladder.

(i) The lining of his stomach would dry out, causing dry heaves and vomiting.

(j) He would develop hyperthermia, a very high body temperature.

(k) His brain cells would begin to dry out, causing convulsions.

(l) His respiratory tract would dry out, giving rise to very thick secretions, which could plug his lungs and cause death.

(m) Eventually his major organs would fail, including his lungs heart and brain." [8]

When a person dies of a disease, he may very well suffer some of the effects in (a) through (m) above. In such cases, medical people used to try to *relieve* his suffering. But now we are looking at inflicting this torture on people who are *not* dying or suffering these symptoms—people whose main problem is that they are physically unable to defend themselves against those who consider their existence a "burden."

In one such case, the parents of a twenty-eight-year-old comatose woman were told by doctors that their daughter would die quickly (within three to nine days) if nourishment were withdrawn.

They then secured a court order to remove her feeding tube—but the daughter frustrated and embarrassed the medicos and the parents by taking 43 days to die.[9]

Forty-three days of a painful, lingering death—all because the parents bought the lie of "painlessly pulling the plug."

Christians cannot accept this as the right way to treat a person.

The Tube Job

Dr. Wolf Wolfensberger, a strong advocate of the rights of the medically dependent, points out, "In a great many 'euthanasia' and voluntary suicide argumentations, it is pointed out that a patient is being tube-fed, and this is used as a death-making argument." But the *facts* about tube-feeding are quite different from what we have been led to believe:

People who have not already embraced a deathmaking mentality need to become aware of the fact that increasingly, stomach tubes are being installed merely as a convenient and less expensive substitute for nursing care. Patients who could manage quite well if they were gently and tediously hand-fed get these tubes installed simply because the modern medical system is not willing to pay for this type of nursing care. In turn, this creates long-term dependencies on tubes, and also raises the likelihood that all sorts of other complications will arise. People on tubes often have diarrhea and infection. The diarrhea often leads to skin ulcers, and the infections often lead to yet other treatments which can be life-endangering. People on stomach tubes are also less likely to be elevated, to be permitted to get out of bed and sit up, and they therefore, are more at risk of beginning to get pretzelled up. In fact, they may be rendered non-ambulatory when, without the tube, they could have been returned to ambulation. People particularly likely to get stomach tubes installed are those who do not recover rapidly after an operation, and who do not have friends and relatives to tend to them in the hospital and to defend them against this kind of medical aggression and deathmaking.[10]

We have already talked a little about the warped medical priorities of modern nursing care. Here is another example of how far we have already slid under the pressure of the New Wave. Patients are put "on the tube" for the *convenience* of the hospital—and then their being on the tube *causes* them to become sicker—and when they get sick enough, the tube is used as an argument for forbidding them *any* nursing care!

Let's Kill Grandma . . . It's the Most Compassionate Thing to Do

Euthanasia is a classic example of how the New Wave works. First, wipe out the old Christian ethic of compassion in favor of a "new" ethic of convenience. Liberally disguise this shift with old words like "compassion." Redefine the old words to reflect the pro-death shift. At the same time, play on the natural human vices of greed and selfishness. Tell us how much trouble it is to save life, and how much nicer it is for the victim to die.

What is happening is that we are being prepared to think of death as a *benefit*, both for the person sacrificed, for his or her relatives, and for society.

Suzanne Fields pointedly remarked in a 1985 column in *Insight* magazine:

The hot trendy topic on talk shows these days, after X-rated lyrics and AIDS, is "how I helped my mother, my wife, my husband (or fill in the blank) die in dignity."

As an accomplice to an assisted suicide or as the person who actually does the deed in what is euphemistically described as "mercy killing," the celebrity slayers seek applause and forgiveness (and maybe a book contract).

Theirs is the confession in the name of "higher good." "Honor thy father and thy mother" becomes "honor their death wish." And the vow "till death do us part" becomes a little less romantic when it means "till I give you a little push."

Some of the confessions are moving and tragic, but all raise more questions than they answer. . . .

Because we hear only the survivor's tale, we have no way to question it. But what if these stories aren't exactly true?

Could it be that these writers actually persuaded their patients that it was in their best interest to die, to diminish doctor and hospital bills, to let the living get on with their lives? Well, could be. If so, would the justification still be there? Or could it be that the ill wife or father was too far gone to make a decision, and husband or daughter decided to do "what's best"?

How would the rest of us respond to the story then? . . .

Today only 10 percent of all Americans believe that children should bear the burden of taking care of their parents. In the mid-1950s, half of all Americans believed that aging parents were a personal responsibility. . . .

Our attitudes toward death and dying, as well as our care for the elderly, become the true test of our civilization. Those who confess to assisted suicide or who call murder a mercy (which is very different from defending a patient's right to refuse treatment) are attempting a climb up a slippery slope.[11]

The burden (expense and sacrifice) of caring for retarded, handicapped, aged, or very ill people also enters the equation. In an upwardly mobile society it is viewed as sheer folly to deny yourself all of the comforts and luxuries you can afford; people who are not useful to you or "wanted" are simply discarded (the cause of a good many divorces as well).

Convenience is becoming an important part of wantedness. Even when the care is paid by insurance, visiting Mom in the nursing home becomes more than one "wants" to bear. With the pressure of being a sick, unwanted, inconvenient burden, is it any wonder that some older people have been pressured into saying they don't want to live?

Then, finally, once God's Spirit has been banished from the field of caring for the ill, the seven evil spirits can return. As Dr. Wolf Wolfensberger has commented with deadly accuracy, "Afflicted people offend the cultural deities of youthfulness, beauty, fun and escape from pain and suffering."[12]

In this New Age, simply to *need* help would be sufficient reason to be denied it.

The New Medical Age Around the World

We don't have to look very far to see how the new pagan mind-set works itself out in practice. Just look at the other nations that are a bit farther down that road.

First, Australia. This is the country where, several years ago, we saw an article suggesting that live aborted babies *ought* to be used in experiments because otherwise they would be "wasted." Several provinces of Australia have also legalized prostitutes soliciting as close as 1,000 feet away from a children's school.

> According to a sympathetic review of a new pro-"euthanasia" book in the Australian newspaper, *The Age,* of May 2, 1987, "euthanasia" is practiced in Australian hospitals "every day."[13]

Next, the mood in Canada. Abortion has now been declared a constitutional right by the Canadian Supreme Court. This undoubtedly relieved the embarrassment surrounding the case of Toronto police constable David Packer, who was suspended from the force for refusing to stand guard duty outside a then *illegal* abortion clinic.

> The Toronto Transit Commission has given Dying with Dignity free advertising space on its buses, street cars, and subways to promote living wills—at the same time as it refused to accept paid *or* unpaid advertisements by a right-to-life association.[14]

Magnet and Kluge [authors of several books on medical ethics] also said that passive euthanasia is already routine at Canadian neonatal units, and that medical details about impaired children are often presented very selectively to parents so as to dispose them towards a deathmaking decision. Nurses are sometimes ordered to administer increasing doses of morphine to kill them even though the babies are not in pain or even awake. The answer which Magnet and Kluge proposed is to be honest and up front—and kill the babies outright instead of being hypocritical and deceptive.[15]

England, once the home of the Methodist revival, now turns its back on the sick elderly—and sometimes gives them a little push over the edge.

Acute health care is commonly withheld from elderly people in England and other European countries. In the US, the director of the Hastings Ethics Center proposed in October 1987 that acute care be withheld from people above 80 in order to stabilize rising health care costs.[16]

Leaders of the nursing profession in Britain are admitting openly that British nurses are often involved in "euthanasia," deliberately shortening life as well as omitting life-prolonging treatments.[17]

In all this, these formerly Christian countries are just following in the illustrious footsteps of the Soviet medical system, as pioneered by the mass-murderer Joseph Stalin. Vladimir Voinovich, an emigré Russian writer, shares a few details of how compassionate Soviet medicine works nowadays:

I had an uncle who lived in one of the provincial capitals in the Ukraine. He fell sick one day, and his family called an ambulance. The ambulance service asked how old he was. Seventy. "We don't take people like that," they said. True, they did finally come after the family made a scene, but by then it was too late . . .

A poor person is better off not bothering with certain serious operations, because a person in recovery needs many rubles in small denominations under his pillow. As soon as the anesthetic wears off, he should reach under his pillow and hand the nurse a ruble. If he wants to rinse out his mouth, that's a ruble; have his bed straightened, another ruble; needs a bedpan, another.

In some hospitals, where the staff has been spoiled, you have to give three rubles. Otherwise, no one will come to help you. A person who has undergone a serious operation might simply not survive the postoperative stage.[18]

But the real prize for systematic death-dealing goes to the Netherlands. As Dr. Wolf Wolfensberger reports:

Euthanasia in the Netherlands: the more one learns about it, the more alarming it gets, Reportedly, there are 3000 registered "euthanasias on request" per year, but a very extensive population survey revealed that the real number must be vastly higher, and some authorities have estimated it to be as high as 20,000 people a year. That would mean that as many as one death in six might now be the result of "euthanasia." Furthermore it appears more and more that . . . there may be a consent in only 10% of cases. Overt or covert support for the practice is such that nothing can be done about it in the courts, Apparently, the largest opposition group consists of elderly people who are afraid not only of having their lives taken, but having them taken secretly. . . .

On May 17, 1987, the *Toronto Star* carried a very substantial article on the trial of two West German physicians for having killed many thousand of handicapped people during World War II. The very same issue carried another lengthy article on "euthanasia" . . . in the Netherlands. According to one survey, about five out of six Dutch physicians have carried out "euthanasia." The issue was dealt with very sympathetically and in a positive light by the *Toronto Star*, and absolutely no connection was made with the German euthanasia era so extensively documented in another article on the very same page of the same issue. [19]

Once medical people get used to their new role as priest-exe-

cutioners, as in the Netherlands, old people and the very sick have
good reason to fear the hospital. The difference between "passive
euthanasia" and "active euthanasia," after all, is only that injecting
poison provides a neater, more pleasant death than forcing a person to die of slow starvation and thirst. For that matter, plunging a
bayonet into the heart of the chosen victim is also a more pleasant—and more honest—death than slow starvation and thirst. Seen
in this light against the backdrop of euthanasia as "good death,"
Hitler and the Nazi Party would indeed be among the greatest do-
gooders of history. Which explains why the German teens quoted
at the beginning of this chapter are beginning to think more favor-
ably of the mastermind of the Holocaust.

Remember what pre-Nazi "guru," doctor of law Karl Binding,
said about how society would "spiral" (a New Age term) back to
wiping out the unwanted:

> As society progresses in a spiral, we will again come to see the
> higher morality of destroying the unfit.[20]

"He Had No Beauty That Men Should Desire Him"—Isaiah 53, Speaking of Jesus Christ

The retarded who fill many institutions are "unwanted."

So are many of the aged and handicapped.

So, for that matter, was Jesus Christ. King Herod, the legal
ruler of the land, determined soon after Jesus' birth that He was a
"burden on society" and took steps to rid the world of him. That
attempt failed; but later the leaders of the Jews and the local
Romans again agreed that Jesus was a burden on society.

That time they crucified Him.

What God Has to Say About All This

> Is this not the kind of fasting I have chosen . . .
> Is it not to share your food with the hungry
> and to provide the poor wanderer with shelter—

when you see the naked, to clothe him,
and not to turn away from your own flesh and blood?
Then your light will break forth like the dawn,
and your healing will quickly appear . . . (Isaiah 58:6-8)

Honor your father and mother, as the Lord your
God has commanded you, so that you may live
long and that it may go well with you in the
land the Lord your God is giving you.
(Deuteronomy 5:16)

Rescue those being led away to death;
hold back those staggering to slaughter.
If you say, "But we knew nothing about this,"
does not he who weighs the heart perceive it?
Does not he who guards your life know it?
Will he not repay each person according to
what he has done? (Proverbs 24:11, 12)

Does "compassion" mean murder or mercy? Does it mean "putting my patients and relatives out of their misery" or does it mean "caring tenderly for my patients and loved ones, making them comfortable and trying to nurture back their health, until such time as God Himself clearly calls them away"? Does it mean "starvation and thirst" or "a cup of cold water in Jesus' name" (Matthew 10:42)?

Jesus Christ, Himself a sacrificial victim on the cross, had good reason for telling us to go and learn what God meant when He said, "I desire mercy, not sacrifice" (Hosea 6:6; Matthew 9:13). Without mercy, there is nothing left *but* sacrifice. When the antisupernaturalists sweep the house clean, as humanists have done in our society, then "seven spirits more evil than the first" inevitably will return to occupy it (Luke 11:26).

There *is* an answer for this evil. But first we need to become aware of just how far things already have gone. See where Breaker Two of the New Wave marriage of science and paganism is taking us in the next section.

PART III: CANNIBAL RITES AND WRONGS

One Small Step for the New Man

"Magic spells complement the effect of medicines and medicines, on the other hand, support the effect of incantations." That is a tenet which . . . is still completely valid in medical practice today.

(Gerhard Venzmer, *5000 Years of Medicine*)[1]

The witch doctor looked from a distance like the other Chol men sweating in the hot sun as they chopped brush to clear a planting field. Light white muslin shirt, open to the waist, and rolled-up muslin pants—nothing there to inspire fear or awe.

But there was a difference. It was in his eyes and in the way he carried himself. Immediately the men stepped back as the witch doctor approached and knelt before the injured man. And when he opened his cloth bag and began his chants, they stepped back even further. . . .

The witch doctor began to chant over the man who had been bitten by the snake. "Snake bite, I speak words for him. Do it for him. Suck it for him; really do it for him!"

As the witch doctor began to find his stride, he lowered and raised his voice in a chanting rhythm . . . "Do it for him! Really do it for him! The juice of the snake, green devil, red devil, red yellow cheek, white yellow cheek, quiet it for him. Only one day I will speak words to it. I will quiet it; I will do it. Six garlic twigs I give to him. I drink the dye of six twigs. Give him, drink it, do it for him, quiet it! Do it for him! Do it! Do it!"

Perspiring heavily, the witch doctor next turned his attention to a man with a deeply cut foot. "Then here's a cut. Six small twigs I bring. Stop up the foot. Do it! Quiet the foot. Do it for the foot. Six spider webs, thus I stop up the foot. Do it really! Blood of all kinds, black blood. It is beginning to stop. The vein was cut; it came out; yes, let it come together."

This scene from Hugh Steven's true book *The Man with the Noisy Heart* does not fill us with reverence for the witch doctor. The fellow sounds rather silly, dancing around waving his twigs and shouting at the spirits to "Do it!" for the snakebite sufferer. We are not upset when missionary John Beekman, the hero of the book, finds it necessary to undermine the witch doctor's hold on the people. In fact, we rather expect it. Confronting and exposing the witch doctor and shaman (more or less gently) is just what missionaries have to do. It's part of their job of leading the people away from their old pagan religion.

What we often fail to grasp is that the "witch doctor" or "medicine man" is truly a doctor and medical man in the tribal people's eyes. He may be a good doctor or a bad doctor (more frequently he is the latter), but a doctor he is. He is simply practicing medicine according to his pagan presuppositions—a fancy way of saying he is a *pagan* doctor.

Besides calling on the demon spirits, the witch doctor also enforces the tribe's taboos. As the channel between men and gods, he keeps the tribe informed of what sacrifices the gods need for what offenses. He also performs the sacrifices, which can range from the merely symbolic (drinking water dyed red to symbolize blood) to animal sacrifice to human sacrifice. He is both doctor and priest rolled into one.

The Doctor as Pagan Priest

Traditionally, the doctor has been a priest. A few quotes from Gerhard Venzmer's history of medicine suffice to prove this point.

> Everything that we now know about those Ancient Mesopotamian doctors demonstrates that, in addition to a mass of demon-worship, magic and enchantment, those ancient practitioners also developed thoroughly rational methods of treating illness.[2]

> [Regarding ancient Chinese medicine] Just as in all other early civilizations, religion, priestcraft, magic and a belief in demons existed in close proximity to each other, for the inscribed bones served the purpose of oracles, by means of which the priest-doctors could consult the gods about a wide variety of infirmities.[3]

> The Vedas [an collection of ancient Indian writings] are of especial interest to the history of medicine because, as the oldest Indian literary monuments, they transmit the earliest information about the diseases of Ancient India and their medical treatment. Once again, a belief in magic, fear of devils and invocations are to the forefront; once again we encounter the view that disease is a punishment for sins committed.[4]

Similar quotes could be produced for the Mayans, Aztecs, Egyptians, and so on. Again, we lie back in our easy chairs, comforted by the knowledge that all this was too long ago and far away to have anything to do with *us*.

Those old pagan days are gone, after all. Surely in our modern scientific age pagan religion and medicine can't mix!

Before we get too comfortable, let's take a second look both at those ancient pagan civilizations and at the history of medicine in our own civilization.

Drugs and Knives

As you research the history of medicine in the ancient world, one fact almost leaps off the page at you—the strong connection between drugs, surgery, and sacrifice. The notoriously sacrifice-minded Vedics of India, for example, "despite a slender knowledge of anatomy, were extremely interested in surgery."[5] A little later we discover the Indians were also remarkably adept druggists, and a little later still we find the Indians have "a thorough knowledge of human anatomy" and that "the medical books of those days, in contrast to earlier times, contain regular instructions for the study of human corpses."[6] Venzmer wonders how the Vedic doctors were able to develop surgery so quickly to such a high degree as their medical texts indicate. Considering the elaborate and gory offerings the Vedics presented their gods, we can perhaps guess how the doctors obtained this knowledge.

Medical practice was also highly developed among the Aztecs, especially their pharmacopeia. "They knew no less than 1,200 medical plants," a disproportionately large number of which were "narcotic and intoxicating drugs."[7] The Inca doctors also had "a considerable knowledge of drugs," and their surgical talents were even superior to those of the Aztecs, including such operations as amputations and trepanations (cutting open the skull of a living patient, supposedly to relieve pressure on the brain).[8]

So those ancient priest-doctors were not only religious ritualists, but *surgeons*. They prescribed drugs, did operations, and billed their patients, just as doctors do today. In the past, at least, pagan religion and medicine certainly *were* able to mix.

A Second Look at Modern Medical History

Modern medicine is usually said to have started with the Greek doctor Hippocrates, the man who framed the famous Hippocratic Oath which modern doctors used to take. Born about 460 B.C., and himself the son of a doctor, Hippocrates tried to separate medicine from religion. A strict rationalist, Hippocrates attacked the idea of disease as inflicted by the gods, and insisted on scientific investigation of the causes of disease. He insisted that doctors should treat each patient as a complete person, and that the doctor's role was to support the natural healing process.

At this stage of Greek medicine, and for a century after, "nobody yet dared to venture near human corpses" out of respect for the dead.[9] But it didn't take long for the lust for scientific knowledge to express itself. In Egypt, the embalmers had been cutting into dead bodies for centuries. Now, under the influence of Hellenism, "Egyptian kings even placed living criminals at the disposal of scientists for anatomical and physiological study."[10] Which means that live men were getting sliced up as a sacrifice to Science.

The Greek doctors invaded and successfully conquered Roman medicine. The most famous of these was Claudius Galenus, known as Galen. A great experimentalist, Galen found himself hogtied by the Roman law against dissecting people, and turned to animals, thus setting back anatomical science for centuries, since Galen was held the foremost medical authority right up until the Renaissance.

Good Nurses, Bad Surgeons

Under Christian rule medical research is said to have come to a standstill. Medical authors blame this on the monks' preference of burying the dead rather than dissecting them. However, the monks partially atoned for this neglect by founding poor-houses, hospitals, and orphanages; for being the first to recognize "the duty of charity even towards hopeless cases"; and by founding more than 15,000 homes for lepers by the fifteenth century.[11] Thus, while surgery diminished, nursing care blossomed. And since most deaths in the Middle Ages can be traced to poor hygiene more than to lack of operations, perhaps we should not condemn the monks too swiftly for their care for the living and respect for the dead. Who knows what their mortality rates would have been if they had had Lysol and toilets?

On the Cutting Edge

The Renaissance brought new advances in medicine, as humanists threw off the yoke of Christian medical ethics. The famous Leonardo da Vinci became a grave robber in order to get the human corpses from which he made his anatomical drawings. Da Vinci had the presence of mind to hide these from public view (they were only discovered at the beginning of this century), so he failed to make a real contribution to medical knowledge in this area.

It remained for Andreas van Wesele, a man who as a child passed his time catching and dismembering animals, to really advance the science of surgery. To supplement his growing knowledge, Andreas would crowd as close as possible to the executions which took place nearby, so as to see as much of the victim's inner parts as possible. Afterwards he collected the dead men's bones and carried them home. Such industry could not go unremarked, and young van Wesele was packed off to medical school at the University of Paris. Here he, like da Vinci, became a grave robber. Thanks to his tireless dissections of the bodies obtained in these midnight excursions, "there came a day when he knew that Galen had never once dissected a human body in his life."[12] Andreas, whose last name had now been Latinized to Vesalius, now had a dilemma; how could he publish his illegal research and undo Galen's errors? Vesalius now had a real stroke of fortune. Emperor Charles V took Paris—and Vesalius' father was field dispenser to the army of Charles!

Under Charles, Vesalius (only twenty-one years old) "received, for the first time, the permission of the university to dissect corpses and hold anatomical lectures."[13] Vesalius soon became a doctor of medicine, and later the personal physician of Charles V. During this time he worked tirelessly at dissection, while a handy scribe made engravings for what turned out to be volume after volume of anatomy texts.

Under Philip II, who was a better Catholic than Charles, Vesalius suddenly found himself deprived of corpses. The tale of Vesalius comes to a sudden end here. Tradition says that he was dissecting a body unlawfully and discovered the person he was cutting up had a beating heart! Somehow the Inquisition got wind of this and arrested Vesalius. Philip II intervened to get Vesalius' sentence lightened to a vow of pilgrimage, and Vesalius ended his life as a shipwreck victim.

*The Righteous Man Is Kind to His Animal, But
the Kindest Acts of the Wicked Are Cruel
—Proverbs 12:10*

The rest of the history of modern surgical research follows in the path charted by Vesalius: dissecting and vivisecting animals, dissecting and vivisecting humans. "Vivisection" means "cutting up while alive," so you can see that medical researchers of this time had indeed come a long way from the old medieval Christian position. One example will show the attitude of these medical pioneers:

> Borelli (who lived from 1608 to 1679) tackled the problem of animal warmth by means of experiments. Like Santorio Santorio, he, too, made use of the thermometer—which had shortly before been invented by his personal friend Galileo—in order to pursue his theories. As animals were not anesthetized, his experiments seem exceptionally cruel, but they at one stroke served to reduce to absurdity the whole rigmarole of the heart as the source of warmth . . .[14]

Let us find out for ourselves if Borelli's experiments only "seemed" cruel or if they *were* cruel. Here is his own report of one such experiment:

> In order to find out the exact degree of warmth of the heart, I opened the breast of a living stag in Pisa and immediately inserted a thermometer into the left ventricle of the heart. I found that the highest temperature of the heart did not exceed 40 degrees, that is to say the degree of the sun in summer. After I had measured the temperature of the liver, and the intestines of the same living stag with similar thermometers, I found that both heart and intestines had the same temperature . . .[15]

Borelli doesn't mention the stag's screaming and its attempts to wrench itself free from its torturer, but that is perhaps not surprising, since he had to focus all his attention on keeping his thermometers gouged into the beast's beating heart, tender intestines, and liver.

For the Benefit of Mankind

The new ethics of medicine, the pursuit of scientific knowledge irrespective of other considerations, came into full bloom in France after the Revolution. This Revolution, which among other things devoted itself to the destruction of all forms of Christian religion, provided both a plentiful supply of corpses and a willingness to use them for the "benefit of mankind." Young Xavier Bichat, another great anatomist, dissected no fewer than 600 such corpses in a single winter. At this time the postmortem examination also came into its own, thanks to the work of Rene Laennec, the inventor of the stethoscope.

By this point, anatomists and surgeons had absolutely no scruples about cutting up people and animals. Vesalius had been driven by a love of cutting obsessive enough to drive him to break the laws of his time, but the new generation of scientists did not even remember a time when any kind of cutting was forbidden. Dissection of the dead was not even an issue. Neither was the use of animals in even the most cruel experiments, such as Emil Behring's attempts to discover a vaccine for diphtheria and Arnold Adolph Berthold's work on developing the science of hormones. Behring killed so many guinea pigs that he had to recycle those who had survived the first round of injections. Berthold's contribution was removing the gonads of young cocks and transplanting them on the cocks' backs or necks. Following in Berthold's footsteps, yet two more Germans, Von Mering and Minkowski, "caused diabetes in dogs by removing the pancreas, then replanted parts of the pancreas in various random places on the dog's body."[16]

Let us see how far we have come. From grave-robbing . . . to animal vivisection . . . to a fascination with research for research's sake. But more is yet to come. The groundwork has been laid for *human* sacrifice.

Consider the definition of human sacrifice presented in the last chapter: "The murder, torture, and/or cannibalism of an innocent person justified as beneficial for the victim, for another person, or for society." Now consider this quote from the end of Venzmer's book, *5000 Years of Medicine:*

> Once the "immunity barrier" is conquered and the rejection reaction arrested, a whole new era of medicine will dawn. For the necessity of having replacement organs constantly available will have the grim consequence of causing a radical revolution in conceptions held hitherto regarding the untouchable nature of the dead . . . In this respect, medical science is already in the middle of the revolution.[17]

Venzmer was writing in 1968 out of a strictly secular perspective. He did not know about the new spiritual forces at work in society in general, and the field of medicine in particular. Had he known, he might have spoken of a New Age rather than a new era.

The revolution is here.

ELEVEN

The Life of the Flesh

*The acceptance of cessation of brain function as death
clearly implies that "non-function," "useless to others,"
and "apparently inevitable death" can be translated into
death, thus only making it easier for more to accept these
pagan approaches to death.*

(Drs. Paul Byrne and Paul Quay,
On Understanding "Brain Death.")[1]

The life of the flesh is in the blood.

(Leviticus 17:11, 14)

A blood vessel has ruptured in his brain. He is quite young yet . . . only forty-two.

His tall muscular frame is stretched out on the operating table, breathing rhythmically, waiting for the surgical team. He looks like a healthy, sleeping man. The highly trained surgeons anxiously wait for the team leader.

After the initial incisions open the chest and the electric saw divides the sternum, the other doctors go to work, as many as eight of them at once, arms and hands inside the chest cavity . . .

❧   ❧   ❧   ❧   ❧

Wait a minute! Inside the *chest* cavity? Wasn't his problem a *brain* aneurysm? What are the doctors doing opening up his chest?

Not what you'd expect. They are *disconnecting his organs* and placing them in dry-ice packed Igloo Playmate picnic coolers.

❧   ❧   ❧   ❧   ❧

Nobody on the surgical team seems to find the procedure at all strange or distasteful. The doctors' only disappointment occurs as a surgical error contaminates the once-perfect, costly liver.

❧   ❧   ❧   ❧   ❧

In an article in *Omni* magazine, writer Kathleen Stein described this rhythmically breathing man being dismembered for his organs.[2] Without so much as skipping a beat she then referred to the man being disassembled as a "cadaver," even while she told us his lungs were still breathing and his heart still beating. Later, to comfort us, she mentioned he had been declared "brain dead."

The Life of the Flesh Is in the . . . Brain Wave?

Brain dead! We are used to hearing this term used as if it meant something absolute (like the law from Mount Sinai) and measurable (like measuring inches with a ruler). But did you know there are currently over thirty sets of criteria for "brain dead" and *none* of them actually means dead?

"Dead" means "the organism is beginning to break down; it is becoming destroyed." But definitions of brain "death" do not deal with the brain beginning to decompose, which everyone could recognize as death. Instead, they talk about "irreversibility" and "cessation of function."

Doctors Paul A. Byrne and Paul M. Quay, in their booklet *On Understanding "Brain Death,"* point out

Now, irreversibility as such is not an empirical concept and cannot be empirically determined. Both destruction of the [brain] and the cessation of its functions are, in principle, directly observable; such observation can serve as evidence. Irreversibility, however, of any kind, is a property about which we can learn only by inference from prior experience. It is not an observable condition. Hence, it cannot serve as evidence, nor can it rightly be made part of an empirical [criterion] for death. . . .

Further, if irreversible cessation of total brain function were the same thing as destruction of the brain, there would be no purpose to any research designed to discover how to turn any current, medically irreversible cessation to function into a reversible one. Yet such research continues to be remarkably fruitful. . . .

For, if "irreversible cessation of total brain function" were merely other words for saying "complete destruction of the entire brain," as Veith et al and many others who continually interchange the two notions must assume, then why would there be the least hesitation on the part of the proponents to drop all reference to "brain function" and to ease their opponents' fears by substituting "complete destruction of the entire brain?" But, in fact, the proponents have vigorously resisted any efforts to make this replacement. Yet surely, no function of a brain could survive that brain's complete destruction. . . .

Those that accept "irreversible cessation of brain function, or functions" as a determinant of death, after making such a determination, indicate that there is now a cadaver. The "cadaver" is then treated "as alive," i.e. the ventilator is continued, postural drainage is used to prevent pneumonia, turning is done to prevent bed-sores, until the time is convenient to remove the vital organs. *A body undamaged, except for destruction of the brain, is a mortally wounded person who, however, is not yet dead.* (Emphasis ours)[3]

Objecting to definitions of brain "death" that involve cessation of function, they say

Were this argument valid, then any cessation of total brain function would be death, by definition. The recoveries of all those who have shown for many hours, even days, no discernible trace of brain function as a result of various depressant poisons or of hypothermia would have been resurrections from the dead. And if it be objected that such people did not really suffer cessation of total brain function but only seemed to, then we are being offered a criterion that is empirically unable to do the very job it was introduced to accomplish. . . .

The editorial comment in *JAMA* on Sept. 3, 1982 includes "[n]ow we are told a brain-dead patient can nurture a child in the womb, which permits live birth several weeks 'post mortem.' Perhaps this is the straw that breaks the conceptual camel's back . . . the death of the brain seems not to serve as a boundary; it is a tragic—untimely fatal loss, but not death itself."[4]

"Brain-dead" women *have* given birth. In fact, "Brain-Dead Woman Gives Birth" was the headline for the following article published in the *Oregonian,* July 31, 1987.

SANTA CLARA, California—Michelle Odette Poole, who captured national attention during week after week inside her brain-dead mother, was delivered without complications Wednesday morning by Caesarean section . . .

The baby's 34-year-old mother, Marie Odette Henderson, suffering from a tumor, was declared brain-dead June 7 after collapsing at the San Francisco elementary school where she taught . . .[5]

We shouldn't need to be told this, but dead women do not carry live babies for weeks inside them. The hospital staff and husband, though, accepting the verdict of "brain-dead," turned off Mrs. Poole's life support systems after the scheduled C-section, which itself was performed weeks before the baby would have been born normally, perhaps in an attempt to save money on Mrs. Poole's nursing care.

Resurrection . . . or Recovery?

The symptoms of brain death can be mimicked for several days by an overdose of Seconal or other barbiturates. Some sets of criteria do not even require an EEG, which would show the presence of electrical activity from the surface of the higher centers of the brain. Most tests are only for specific visible responses to stimuli. If brain dead equals dead, then regaining consciousness after you have been declared brain dead means you were resurrected—a miracle like Jesus coming out of the tomb. Yet this occurs regularly!

> Doctor Safar in Critical Care Medicine reported on forty patients who were treated for barbiturates. Twenty-two of these had an arrest time lasting between five and twenty-two minutes. The expected neurological recovery would be less than 10%. However, fourteen of the twenty-two (64%) made complete neurologic recovery.
>
> The reason that *recovery is possible is because there was cessation of brain function and not destruction.* . . .
>
> For example, one out of every 12 patients declared dead by the Minnesota or the British criteria or by Guidelines published last year in support of the Uniform Determination of Death Act, now so strongly urged upon state legislatures and courts, still shows non-random functioning of the cortex of the brain—the part where sensation, feeling and consciousness seem to reside.[6]

On the simplest level, brain "dead" patients are not dead because their spirits have not yet left their bodies. Even Kathleen Stein's "Last Rights" article in *Omni* magazine, which was sympathetic to declaring people dead when they are not, included these observations:

> Youngner also talks about the "spirit" the staff often say they feel in the operating room during surgery, the presence of a life-force there but sleeping. O.R. personnel "often feel a similar presence with brain-dead patients, and it doesn't depart until the respirator is turned off." Families talk about spiritual entities as well. Sometimes, says Davis, "they know when their loved one is dead while we're still figuring it out by tests. They know he's just not there anymore."[7]

Meet the "Neo-Morts"

The very idea that lack of measurable brain function is the same as death comes from an atheistic view of man as the most highly evolved animal, only different from other animals because of our superior brains. In contrast, the Bible says, "The life of the flesh is in the *blood*," clearly indicating that as long as blood is moving through your veins, you are alive. Thus, the forty-two-year-old ripped apart for his organs *was* alive according to Scripture—just as any reasonable person observing this man breathing would assume. In the same way, anencephalic babies (babies born with missing brain portions) are alive, and retarded people are alive, and comatose people are alive—the very same people now called "brain dead."

These people who are alive but tagged "brain dead" have been called "neo-morts" (the new dead). Before death was redefined, they were called "alive." Already pressure is building to exploit these alive, but not socially functional, people as organ farms.

The Cutting Edge

Robert L. Olive, 27, became just such an organ farm after he attempted to rob an apartment in early December of 1985 and was shot in the face. Within forty-eight hours he was declared brain dead and his heart was beating in another man.[7] I (Paul) remember seeing the news on television from the first story, which covered the shooting incident. Subsequently it was reported that his mother had signed permission to donate his organs. The TV scene showed Olive being wheeled into the hospital wearing, not a ventilator, which would breathe for him, but an oxygen mask . . . meaning he was breathing on his own. The final story was of the "successful" transplant and how happy the recipient was to have lived so others might die.

Some might find little sympathy and even see some poetic justice for this thief whose heart was stolen. Please remember that Robert Olive was *never found guilty* of his crime—a crime which has *never been capital,* in any case. He was not a mass murderer convicted in a court of law. Robert Olive was sentenced to death for being a *defenseless tissue match.*

Abusing criminals and suspects may be quite an effective way to desensitize the public to the maltreatment of other "unwanted" people. When *should* someone be sentenced to being an organ donor? For murder? . . . rape? . . . robbery? . . drunk driving? . . . non-payment of taxes? . . . three parking tickets?

Higher Consciousness, Lesser Lives

While some balk at the idea of measurable brain function defining life and death, many, such as neurologist Fred Plum of Cornell University Medical College, feel we should go even further. Dr. Plummer has said that *self-awareness* should be the definition of life:

> "I believe that the meaning of life is cognition and self-awareness, not merely visceral survival. The concept holds that when the cognitive brain has departed, the person has departed."[9]

What he is really saying is that if the person cannot respond in ways that satisfy us, then he is dead. Dr. Plummer went on to explain that this a personal, not a medical, opinion. But when someone in his position expresses an opinion on a medical subject, it has the effect of encouraging the public to adopt the doctor's opinion.

Who is self-aware, anyway? What about the mentally retarded? Someone who is not an initiate into Eastern religious thought, who has not attained "self realization" or "true enlightenment," is considered not to be self-aware. What of those asleep? . . . under anesthetic? . . . drugged or drunk? . . . unconscious? . . . in a coma? What about those who can walk and talk but have not attained New Age "cosmic consciousness"? Who is going to define self-awareness . . . and where will they stop?

Richard M. Burcke, a Canadian psychiatrist, wrote in 1901 that "a time will come when to be without the faculty of Cosmic Consciousness will be a mark of inferiority."[10] His book, *Cosmic*

Consciousness, is now hailed as a New Age classic. What does that tell us about redefining life as self-awareness?

Yes, He's Screaming, But He Doesn't Feel It

To see what difference the doctrine of self-awareness makes, consider how doctors who believe babies are not self-aware have been treating them for years. *Insight* magazine ran an article on pain perception in newborns that generated letters for many issues following.[11] Research, it turns out, shows that preemies and newborns subjected to operations without anesthesia show high symptoms of stress and have difficulty recovering.

One of us (Mary) personally observed this when my first baby was in New York Hospital's intensive care unit. A baby recently operated on was screaming in obvious pain. The nurse assured the anxious parents that it was OK and that the baby would receive painkillers. After the parents left, one nurse told the other in an undertone that she thought it was horrible that the doctors wouldn't use anaesthesia in an operation on a baby such as that, and afterwards wouldn't let her give the poor, suffering babies "as much as an aspirin!" She was so agitated that she repeated the last phrase "Not even as much as an aspirin!" several times. It also upset her that she was expected to lie to the parents and tell them that their babies *were* getting pain relief. This did not make *me* feel too good, as my own son had been operated on in that hospital!

However, in spite of the research and the obvious screaming, etc. of babies cut open without anesthesia, several learned people took it upon themselves to write long letters stating that babies as old as a year and three months (old enough to walk, if they are healthy) can't "perceive" pain.[12]

Wanted babies have difficulty getting treated as people; aborted babies do not qualify today for any consideration whatsoever. Not only are they ripped, burned, torn and poisoned to death, but now some are kept alive to be used in painful and gruesome experiments or freeze-dried and made into jewelry, encased in plastic and sold as paperweights, ground up and used for cosmetics, tattooed and used as "art," and "harvested" for tissue and organ transplants.[13]

New work is going forward using the young, adaptable pancreas cells from aborted babies to install a working pancreas into diabetics. We are promised that this will result in diabetics who no longer need insulin. Babies' brain cells are being used as replacements for damaged portions of the brain to treat Parkinson's disease.[14]

Joseph Fletcher, father of situation ethics, has no qualms about such bizarre activities. He says, "I don't see how rights apply to *potential humans,* therefore, because *I don't assign human status* to fetal life, I see no ethical objection to using fetal tissue in transplants."[15]

"Potential humans." That live, breathing baby is a "potential human" who, according to Joseph Fletcher, can be cut up for transplants. Do you see where the use of loaded terms like "brain dead" and "self-aware" is leading us?

"These Pagan Approaches to Death"

Doctors Byrne and Quay say, "While transplantation and the advancement of science are, in general, commendable and often highly emotional issues, it is not acceptable to remove a vital organ from someone, who, if he is not yet dead, will be killed by the excision of the vital organ." Unhappily, as they are keenly aware, their voice has not prevailed.

As Willard Gaylin wrote in *Harper's Magazine* in Sept. 1974, "The problem (of euthanasia) is well on its way to being resolved by what must have seemed a relatively simple and ingenious method. As it turned out, the difficult issues of euthanasia could be evaded by redefining death." . . .

While death with dignity, living will and assisted suicide must be vigorously resisted, the acceptance of cessation of brain function as death clearly implies that "non-function," "useless to others," and "apparently inevitable death" can be translated into death, thus only making it easier for more to accept these *pagan approaches to death.*[16]

"These pagan approaches to death" are being implemented more and more vigorously . . . with surprisingly little resistance so far, as you will see.

TWELVE

The Body Snatchers

To eat the victim is a convenient means of disposal, a
useful alternative to burning or burying him alive.
(Nigel Davies)[1]

On a less "spiritual" basis, it was the practice in many
regions to eat a certain part of a healthy man's corpse in
order to cure the corresponding part that was diseased in
a living man
(Garry Hogg, Cannibalism and Human Sacrifice)[2]

I think there is sufficient evidence to prove that, when
men offer the lives of their fellow-men in sacrifice to
their gods, they do so as a rule in the hopes of thereby
saving their own.
(Edward Westmarck,
researcher on human sacrifice)[3]

With great advances in life-support technology and
organ transplantation, the dead today do indeed have
much 'protein' to offer us—in the form of their organs
and body parts. We are the neo-cannibals.
(Nobel Prize winner Carleton Gajdusek)[4]

They said he was dead.

Still, as I (Mary) scanned the newspaper, I saw something that made me stop reading in a hurry and backtrack through that article.

It was the two words "oxygen mask."

The story went something like this. A man from one state had been declared dead. However, his relatives were willing to donate one of his essential organs (heart? liver? I don't remember) to an ill person needing the transplant in another state. So the "dead" man, accompanied by a nurse and *wearing an oxygen mask,* was flown by airplane to the other hospital. There the operation was performed—successfully, I believe—and the dead man dropped out of the picture.

I had read articles like this hundreds of times before. So have you. What made me sit up and take notice was that here, for the first time, the newspaper reporter had artlessly informed us all that the "dead" man was in fact alive and breathing on his own.

Dead men, you see, wear no oxygen masks.

Sitting there, I translated the story to myself. A live human being, breathing but incapacitated, had been artificially labeled "dead." He then had been flown, *still breathing,* to another location, where at the request of his near and dear his body was cut open—while his heart was beating—and his organs sliced out, thereby causing his for-real death.

All of a sudden I had a lot of questions for that newspaper reporter.

Who had said that man was dead?

Why did they say that?

Did they at least *give him anesthesia* when they cut the heart out of his living body? (Not likely, since after all he was "dead" and since anesthesia could make his donated organ less viable.)

How could his *relatives* agree to this?

How could that *nurse* sit next to an innocent live human being and blithely conduct him to his execution?

And last, but not at all least—*why had nobody ever told us that they were killing breathing people for their body parts?*

Transplant Cannibalism

Nobel Prize-winning virologist Carleton Gajdusek found a cannibalistic rite among the Fore people of New Guinea which was responsible for the spread of a virus among that people. He also found a novel interpretation of cannibalism and its uses today.

Kathleen Stein reports in *Omni* magazine:

It was Gajdusek's opinion that were it not for the viral infection in the tissue, eating brains would have "provided a good source protein for a meat starved community." Not long after I started this story, I went to hear Gajdusek speak at Mt. Sinai Hospital in New York. During the address he spoke of the "neocannibalism" of modern medicine.

"With great advances in life-support technology and organ transplantation, the dead today do indeed have much 'protein' to offer us—in the form of their organs and body parts. *We are the neo-cannibals.*" (emphasis ours)[5]

We didn't say it first. A Nobel Prize winner said it. When we take apart a person, alive or dead, for his tissue or organs, *we are the neo-cannibals.*

The very term "to cannibalize" means "to take apart for parts." Human cannibalism has always meant *eating* or otherwise *ingesting* another person's body—whether directly through the mouth or injected into the bloodstream. It can also mean *taking in a part of his body* directly into your own body against the "donor's" will or in such a way that the "donor" is killed by this exchange.

All these forms of cannibalism are now reviving in our newly paganized culture.

You Are What You Are Eating

We apologize in advance for the stories that are about to follow. They are gruesome by anyone's standard, and we would spare you them if we could. But this is real life; it's really happening today, and if we don't stop it, it will keep on happening tomorrow.

First, we are moving back to eating human flesh. As Frank Farmer wrote in his January 25, 1987 newspaper column:

It is acceptable to splice a gene from another plant into a tomato or strawberry plant to gain a beneficial trait, such as nitrogen fixation or frost tolerance. But it is quite something else when these scientists start mixing human and animal genes. And that is what is going on—of all despicable things in, of all places, the hallowed USDA Experimental Station in Beltsville, Md.

At Beltsville, our wondrous tax-supported employees inserted a human gene that controls growth into a pig's cell. The pig was thus described: "The pig with human genes seldom gets up. The boar, bigger-snouted and hairier than usual, lies in his pen despite the nudgings of a normal pig put in for company. But Pig No. 32, a 400 pound boar, implanted with human growth genes, has sired many of the pigs in the experiments, passing the genes on to his offspring."

I would suggest that animals such as Pig 32 be slaughtered and that experiments cease.[6]

Commenting on the tale of Pig 32, farm photojournalist and researcher C. F. Marley said:

Our government is against leaded gas because we get lead in the atmosphere in parts per billion; it worries about pesticides in fish when they are measured in parts per billion; it worries about any kind of water contamination where it can be measured in parts per billion.

But what about splicing human genes into hogs? [In 1975 there were 2,336 recognized Mendelian traits in humans, which might with fair accuracy be called synonymous with "genes." Assuming hogs and other mammals have about the same number of genes, then] it looks to me like we have a human contamination of hogs at about 4 parts per ten thousand.

A most repulsive thought occurred to me but I thought I might be a little supersensitive. Then I discussed this matter with a friend, and his comment was that it all sounded a little bit cannibalistic.

There can be no justification for this kind of research.[7]

"I'll Fight the Yankees, But I Ain't Gonna Eat 'Em!"

As so often happens, it remains to those who lived and died before our "modern" age to write the fitting epitaph to this great new advance in livestock management. Franklin Sanders, in his *Moneychanger* newsletter, passes on a story that Mr. Richard Kelly

Hoskins of Lynchburg, Virginia, heard about his grandfather during the Civil War.

> At the battle of Cross Keys his Confederate unit was pinned down by heavy Yankee fire from across a ridge. Many Yankees lay dead directly in front of them. As Hoskins' grandfather's unit crouched there, pigs came out of the woods and began to gnaw at the dead. Later, after the battle, someone offered him a piece of ham. He looked at him askance and said, "I don't mind *killing* Yankees, but I'm d—d if I'm gonna *eat* 'em!"[8]

A similar instance was reported by a young Revolutionary War soldier. After a battle, hogs were observed devouring the dead. Due to the Christian ethic of those days, even though times were tough and fat pigs were abundant in that area (their fatness partly due to their high-protein diet of dead soldiers), nobody was willing to engage in cannibalism by eating hogs that had eaten humans.

Franklin Sanders perceptively points out:

> The gruesome remembrance comes to me that New Guinea cannibals refer to their unnatural feast as "long pig." . . . This ultimate infamy [of raising part-human pigs for food] is only the logical progeny of a government and a culture that has replaced the Law of God with the "law" of autonomous man. After all, if you can kill upwards of 20 *million* unborn children by abortion and use their bodies to make cosmetics, and propagandize the killing of old folks as "merciful," then it is not God but man who makes the ultimate rule. So why not splice human genes into hogs and eat the cursed pork? Why just splice in one or two genes? Why not just kill the humans outright, slaughter them, send the meat to the supermarket, and skip the middleman hog? Dean Swift's *Modest Proposal* [an essay satirizing the eighteenth-century English upper class's callous attitude towards the poor by suggesting that the problem of poverty be solved by eating the poor] was just 200 years ahead of its time.[9]

My Mother the Chimp

In this almost-New Age of medicine, researchers are going farther than splicing human genes into hogs to produce bigger, more tasty hogs. They would like to create a new race of sub-men:

> Italian scientists reportedly have experimented secretly on attempts to cross-fertilize humans and chimpanzees with a view to creating an anthropoid slave class or a pool of organ sources. These efforts are vastly more sophisticated than those first reported to be carried out in Paris in the mid-1930s with what were described as "the most crude methods," which we can well imagine what they were.[10]

"Everyone Experiments on Them"

But, since regular human beings are now considered "medical resources," perhaps the Italian researchers are simply behind the times. Coma victims, for example, are already surreptitiously cannibalized for research.

> The Seattle *Times* in 1985 reported that: "A team of doctors has acknowledged it performed an experimental blood transfusion on a man in an irreversible coma without notifying his family."
>
> It quoted one doctor as saying: "In any case, everyone more or less already experiments on these patients" . . .[11]

As Kathleen Stein reported in *Omni* magazine,

> The French, who claim to be horrified at discontinuing treatment of long-term vegetatives, in the same breath advocate using them experimentally . . .[12]

You could call this attitude a lot of things, but "slavery" about sums it up. Just as pagan societies generally kept slaves, who were the first and most natural choice for sacrificial victims, today the medically dependent are increasingly considered to *belong* to the hospital. This raises entirely new possibilities in the areas of long-term torture, since these people are often "biologically tenacious" (which means they live a long time in spite of the care they receive) and conscious of their surroundings, even though they are unable to defend themselves. In any case, it seems we already have our "inferior class" right there in the hospital bed—people who are considered the legitimate prey of the wealthy, healthy, and depraved.

Have a Heart?

German scholar Edward Westmarck, in his *Origin and Development of the Moral Ideas,* a work which dealt, among other things, with the reasons for human sacrifice, had this to say:

> The custom of human sacrifice admits that the life of one is taken to save the lives of many, or that an inferior individual is put to death for the purpose of preventing the death of somebody who has a higher right to live.[13]

Now consider this item appearing in Wolf Wolfensberger's *TIPS* newsletter:

> David Schwartz recently sent us an appeal by a Yale University professor for a person to donate his/her heart to a prominent colleague. The appeal was headed, "Dr. so-and-so needs a heart and your help."[14]

Obviously the drafter of that appeal felt that Dr. So-and-So had a higher value than whoever would be sacrificed to save him. Not only that, he honestly believed the readers of that letter would agree with him that someone else ought to die to save the eminent doctor!

Your Duty to Donate

Just as in the ancient pagan world the poor had a "duty" to die if the rich wanted to cannibalize them for food or medicine, now we are being told that we have a "duty" to donate our organs (which, remember, are removed from our *living* bodies) if another, more socially useful person "needs" them. As an impassioned article appearing in the usually sensible *Freeman* journal of the Foundation for Economic Education cried:

> According to recent reports, the black market value of a kidney which can be transplanted is some $13,000—which translates to roughly seven times its weight in gold. This is a dramatic figure, and behind it lies a tale of untold human suffering.

> Whose human suffering? Not the suffering of those whose kidneys are extracted to be sold on the black market . . .

> There are thousands of people who *desperately* need kidney transplants. Paradoxically, there are other thousands of people who die each year, taking healthy kidneys to the grave. . . . Why, it may be asked, cannot potential donors be given a pecuniary reward for doing the *right thing?*

> The writer then argues emotionally that noncoercive pleas for donations are not yielding the required amount of kidneys.

> Things have reached such a pass that in Canada there are plans being bruited about which would allow the government to seize the kidneys of accident victims unless they have signed cards denying such permission. . . .
>   It is time to put aside our archaic and prejudicial oppositions to the marketplace, so that we can relieve the suffering and, in many cases, *lift the death sentence we have inadvertently placed on our fellow citizens.* (emphasis ours)[15]

Compulsory Cannibalism

Note how refusing to donate your kidneys, or those of your loved ones, is now termed "placing a death sentence" on potential kidney recipients. Since murder is illegal, if refusing to donate can be relabeled "murdering needy transplant recipients," refusal to donate could be made illegal. Never mind that removing the kidney for transplant *actually* "places a death sentence" upon the so-called donor (you're not really a donor if *someone else* gives away your organs) who "desperately needs" medical care!

Kathleen Stein gives us a glimpse of the future in *Omni:*

> The radical, outspoken Dr. Tellis is concerned with life, the hanging-by-a-thread life of someone waiting for a heart or liver or kidney. He has no patience with families who refuse to donate the organs of brain dead (Note: "brain dead" *not* "dead") kin. The *social climate* surrounding donation today should be reversed, he told me as he waited at Good Samaritan Hospital that night for the rest of the transplant surgeons to arrive for R.H.'s organs. "Instead of feeling good and righteous about donating," he said, "it should enter the collective unconscious that you feel bad if you refuse. The family who refuses to donate a dead (Note: the switch in terminology from "brain dead" to "dead") relative's liver *should be told they killed the waiting recipient!*" (parentheses and emphases ours)[16]

Tellis is not satisfied that some people *willingly* donate organs, nor that they even be allowed to feel good about it but that they should be *coerced* to donate, at which point it ceases to be a donation. Quite beyond this he insists that we rearrange the *social climate* to produce guilt in those who choose not to be dismembered. Considering the vehemence of his remarks, a suggestion of changes in the legal climate cannot be far off. In fact, there is *already* a federal law *requiring* doctors to ask for organ donations:

> The law, which took effect Thursday, requires hospitals that receive Medicare and Medicaid funds to ask the families of

deceased or comatose patients whether the patients' organs could be used for transplants. The law was meant to overcome a reluctance by medical people to intrude on families' grief in asking for organ donations. . . .

When a family member dies, she said, the idea of donating organs frequently doesn't occur to relatives. "By the time they think about it the time limits for donations might well have elapsed," she said. . . . Organs are not normally removed unless recipients are waiting for them. Kidneys can be kept for 48 hours between removal and transplant; hearts, four hours, livers, six hours. Other tissues—skin, bone and eyes— can be kept much longer outside the body. Eyes can be preserved for five days. Skin and bone can be kept frozen up to two years. . . .

The new federal law is welcomed by the American Council on Transplantation, which estimates as many as 25,000 Americans die each year in ways that would permit their hearts, livers and kidneys to be transplanted, even though 40 other states now have some sort of donor-notification law. Arthur Harrell, spokesman for the organization, said only 17 percent to 20 percent of those potential donors now actually have their organs removed.[17]

Again, the article talked about how long the hearts, livers, and so on could be kept outside the body, but did *not* mention that they have to be removed from a *living* human being in order to be useful in the first place. Also note that patients are now being looked at as "potential donors," and tallies are being kept of what percentage of these "potential donors" actually end up losing their organs—strongly implying that 100 percent "donation" would be ideal.

In other countries, human sacrifice *is* now required. Belgium, for instance:

A new Belgian law allows human organs to be taken for transplant without direct consent. The measure is the country's answer to a shortage of donated organs.[18]

Or how about this news item from Brazil:

In Taubate, Brazil, local doctors have been accused of removing organs from living as well as dead patients and selling them to hospital transplant teams in Sao Paulo. The regional medical council and the local police are investigating 11 doctors.

In one instance, 11-year-old Sylvia Moura was hospitalized with a broken leg and came home with a kidney removed.

In another case, the family of a 15-year-old boy, Helder Faria, who was in a coma, was visited by a woman claiming to be a "parapsychologist." She told them she had conversed in her mind with the boy and he had appealed to his parents to give his organs *because only in this way would his life have continuity.*

The boy's kidneys, corneas, liver and heart were removed and, obviously, he died. (emphasis ours)[19]

But really, the Brazilian doctors were just following the famous law of supply and demand. Someone with money wanted an organ, so they stole one for him. In doing this, they were merely entrepreneurs slightly in advance of the legal market. Kathleen Stein notes the economic pressures which could make organ-snatching legal:

Over the next 20 years, the overwhelming demand for organs may increase the pressure to simply declare the "brain absent" dead. There is already something of a black market for buying and selling organs. If the cognitive-death definition were instituted, organ merchandising corporations might establish enterprises beyond Wall Street's wildest insider fantasies. The world would find itself in a situation where death itself would be an industry—an economic incentive.[20]

As Garry Hogg, author of *Cannibalism and Human Sacrifice*, perceptively noted,

Once give a religious, or magical, or pietistic excuse for the devouring of fellow human beings, and the demand inevitably grows and grows; and supply must follow demand.[21]

Hogg could just as well have said, "Once give a *medical* or *economic* excuse for the devouring of human beings." But maybe he was right after all; for medicine and economics seem to be dovetailing with Hindu (New Age) paganism these days.

What is behind this headlong rush toward surgical cannibalism? Is it just rigorous "scientific" humanism—considerations of costs and benefits? Or is some more sinister force at work . . . like the New Age belief in reincarnation through sacrifice expressed by the Brazilian parapsychologist who talked that poor boy's family into cutting him up as a human sacrifice?

Carol Everett, former owner of abortion mills in Dallas, Texas, was asked what got her out of the abortion business. Her testimony reveals there is more to the pro-death movement than meets the eye.

She related how a Dallas preacher felt that the Lord was calling him to go into her abortuary to bring someone out. After several conversations with Everett, and after much prayer, she decided to leave the abortuary. "There is not a thing that happens in an abortion mill that is not a lie," she said. "A tremendous number of lesbians work at the clinics. *There is a definite link between abortion mills and the occult. People involved in abortion are involved in demonic activity.*" Everett said that the presence of even one picketer "shines a light" inside the abortion mill.[22]

Now the following report by a San Antonio sidewalk counselor makes a bit more sense:

"I could hardly believe my eyes when an employee at New Women's Clinic [an abortion clinic] showed up on Halloween dressed as a witch, complete with gruesome make-up and a bracelet of human-looking eyeballs."[23]

Who Will be the Next Victims?

So we have this interesting situation: a huge demand for organs, which can only be removed exactly when the recipient needs them, and a quite natural shortage of people who can be convincingly labeled "brain dead" so their organs can be harvested.

Classic economic theory would say that the next step would be for some enterprising businessman, or for the government, to meet the demand for organs by creating a supply of people from whom these organs could be removed.

Now, who might these involuntary sacrificial victims be?

Wolf Wolfensberger offers some insight into that question.

An interesting and as yet virtually unremarked phenomenon is occurring in our society. On the one hand, people who commit offenses of civil disobedience in response to the dictates of their conscience—offenses which often involve merely symbolic actions or minor property damage—are being subjected to extremely severe punishments, with additional severity in denial of parole or pardons. We have already cited Helen Woodson in past TIPS issues as one example; she received an 18-year sentence for entering a nuclear missile base and striking some of the armaments with hammers. Another example is a woman who did no more than enter a Florida abortion clinic in an attempt to unplug a suction machine. She was sentenced to five years in prison in 1986, and even put into solitary confinement. The very same judge who sentenced her on the very same day sent two men convicted as accessories to murder to four-year prison terms. On the other hand, people who commit the most heinous crimes of violence, both in the destruction of property and the destruction of humans, either receive relatively light sentences, or are paroled in relatively short order.

Once a pattern like this begins to emerge, it is really urgent that we understand the underlying meaning and message. . . . Acts of civil disobedience . . . however small, are correctly perceived by [the power elite] as a challenge to its very nature, existence, and assumptions. They proclaim that [the elite] consciousness is not a valid one, nor even the only one, and that it is possible to become freed of imperial controls over the mind and soul.

In the perception of the empire, *that* is much more dangerous than a little murder, robbery, or arson, because if *that* spreads, then other subjects will also throw off their chains.[24]

We have already seen in an earlier chapter how accused thief Robert Olive was seized and harvested for his organs. This would parallel the ancient Greek practice of preferring criminals as sacrificial victims. The question then is, *what kind of criminals* would be likely to suffer this fate in a medical/political establishment run according to pagan New Age thinking?

If Wolfensberger is right—and the trend in court sentences certainly confirms his thinking—*dissenters* would be those voted Most Likely to Decease.

Now, who is most likely to be considered a dissenter in a New Age order?

You figure it out.

THIRTEEN

And They Sacrificed Their Children to Molech

A Winnipeg (Ontario, Canada) surgeon recently announced that, "I will do what the Aztecs did," meaning cutting out the still-beating heart of an anencephalic infant to be given to another infant.

(*TIPS*, April 1988)

I don't think these kids are dead, But would I take the organs out? Yes.

(Art Caplan, director of the Center for Bio-Medical Ethics at the University of Minnesota)[1]

I've been asked if I could actually cut up this baby, take the organs, and put them in another baby. My answer is, 'Yes, I could.'

(Brenda Winner, mother of an anencephalic baby)[2]

The Leopard Men crouched in the brush. All was in readiness. The girl's father and mother had been visited, and had agreed to her sacrifice. Truly, they had had no choice, for had not Yongolado told them the sacrifice was needed for the good of the tribe? Now they waited in the dark for the girl, just in her teens.

Her feet scrunching in the leaves of the forest floor, Piki stepped carefully down the trail. Why had her parents told her to go down this path alone, at night, and bring back an herb which

132

anyone could have gathered in the broad daylight? She felt a thrill of fear.

Suddenly the jungle erupted in deep-throated growls. Piki stood still, frozen in horror, as Yongolado leaped upon her. Leopard Men! They crowded around her and pulled her deeper into the jungle, while one remained behind to make the leopard prints leading away from the trail the group was taking.

Almost dead with fright, Piki sat stunned as the Leopard Men tied her to a tree. Ignoring her pleading cries, the chief came forth and straddled her shoulders, while the others thronged to touch her or the chief for a blessing.

Yongolado offered a prayer for good medicine and tore out her throat.

He then sliced Piki open.

Another Leopard Man leaped forward. Leaning out, he stuck his hand into Piki's belly and ripped out her intestines and liver.

Still another Leopard Man pulled out some fat.

Piki lived yet a while longer . . .

When her blood had stopped flowing, the organs were taken away to be made into medicine.

On the next day, Piki's body was ceremonially cut up as a feast for the tribe. Her own parents were at this feast and were given portions as a reward.(Adapted from actual accounts of cannibalism among the Leopard Men of Sierra Leone, as reported by Garry Hogg, *Cannibalism and Human Sacrifice*.)[3]

❦   ❦   ❦   ❦   ❦

The Leopard Men of Sierra Leone horrify us with their bloodthirstiness. But these cultists had *genuine medical reasons* for their gruesome behavior. Researcher Garry Hogg reports,

Questioned, tribesmen have declared emphatically that their reason for killing and devouring human beings is to create a powerful medicine, the *borfimor* . . .[4]

Now, this *borfimor* may or may not be effective for its purpose. But the tribesmen's motives are the classic motives of human sacrifice: "The murder, torture, and/or cannibalism of an innocent person justified as beneficial for himself, for another person, or for society."

Here is another story of human sacrifice from a somewhat more recent period:

❦ ❦ ❦ ❦ ❦

The baby lay defenseless on the table. Her heart was beating; she might have breathed on her own, had the doctors not put her on a respirator so as to be able to declare her "brain dead" later when they turned off the respirator.

Finally, the moment came.

While the baby's heart continued to beat, a doctor sliced open her belly.

Sticking his hand into her belly, he pulled out and carefully removed her kidneys and liver.

The baby was still alive. In fact, she *had* to remain alive for the rest of the operation to be successful. A machine would breathe for her, in order to keep her from dying—other machines would keep her blood moving, if necessary.

Working even more quickly, the doctor tied off and cut out her beating heart.

At a more leisurely rate, his assistants then sliced out the baby's corneas and any other parts that seemed salvageable.

❦ ❦ ❦ ❦ ❦

You have just read a description of the new "miracle" medical procedure known as "harvesting anencephalic babies for their organs." Anencephalic babies are a transplant surgeon's dream come true. Born with a brain stem, but not enough of a brain to stay alive for very long, these children are being promoted as the newest source for organs for transplant. Thanks to our society's unbiblical preoccupation with brain function as the definition of humanness, these children are on the verge of being declared "brain absent" at birth, meaning that they do not even have to be declared "brain dead" before a surgeon can be in there cutting them to pieces. And, exactly as with the Leopard Men cult, parents are being prepared to actually *offer* these children for living death.

(10-29-87) For many years, physicians have sought an ethically justifiable way to obtain organs from the 2,000 to 3,000 infants born every year with virtually no brain, a condition termed anencephaly. Because they do have a primitive brain stem that allows them to breathe on their own for a few days, but rarely longer, such infants do not qualify as "brain dead" until breathing ceases. . . .

Dr. Timothy Frewen of University Hospital in London, Ontario, said that doctors had passed a "milestone" by using life-support equipment to benefit not the anencephalic baby but another who would receive her heart. He said in a telephone interview that he believed the strategy had opened the door to more widespread use of anencephalic babies as organ donors. And, he added, it also gives comfort to parents of lethally deformed infants because their child can "make a significant contribution to life."

But others were disturbed.

"I'm very bothered by this," said George Annas, professor of public health at Boston University. "The question is: 'Is this a baby or not?' At its starkest, these children are not being treated as human beings but as organ banks.". . .

Dr. Ron Cranford, a Minneapolis neurologist who is president of the American Society of Law and Medicine, said he believed that it would eventually be permissible to remove organs from anencephalics while they were still breathing. "It is not really possible to declare a child under 7 days brain dead," he said. "I say we have to be upfront about what we are doing."

Arthur Caplan, a bioethicist at the University of Minnesota, agrees, saying that what was done in Canada has something of a charade quality to it because the doctors are covering themselves legally in a way that smacks of technical trickery.[5]

When They Who Have Not the Law Obey the
Law, They Show That the Law Is Written on
Their Hearts (After Romans 2:14, 15)

You would expect Christians to have risen up at once to condemn these pagan sacrifices. But so far this has not happened. The first (and originally only) hospital in the United States willing to harvest anencephalic babies is Loma Linda University Medical Center in California, a supposedly "Christian" Seventh-Day Adventist institution.

In cases such as this, sometimes unbelievers put us to shame. Even syndicated columnist Ellen Goodman, not exactly a pro-life activist by anyone's definition (she has consistently promoted abortion and "death with dignity"), is appalled at the idea of cutting the living heart out of these children. She points out, "Anencephalic newborns are not brain dead by our current definition. They have a brain stem. They can breathe and blink and maybe suckle."[6]

The authors of this book first heard about this horrible new medical practice when one of us was being interviewed on a California talk show. A news report aired just before the show described (nonjudgmentally) how a mother wanted to offer her baby as an organ bank and told us that Loma Linda Hospital had agreed to do the job. When airtime came, I volunteered to debate anyone from Loma Linda Hospital who cared to defend this practice. When, predictably, hospital personnel were unwilling to try to defend cutting open little babies in a debate with someone who actually opposed the practice, we began to pray that God would spare this baby the horrors of being cut open while alive.

God answered those prayers.

The baby girl lived beyond the artificial seven-day limit during which she could be "harvested," thus, in the words of another newspaper article, "dashing [the mother's] hopes" that she might be able to redeem her social sin of conceiving an imperfect baby by sacrificing her living child on a medical altar.

"I Knew I Had to Terminate the Pregnancy": An Exercise in Motherly Love

Why is it that *mothers* are now at the forefront of the crusade for infant sacrifice? One such mother, Gail Marell of California, shares her thought processes as she discovered her unborn baby was anencephalic.

As [the doctor] explained our options I knew that I had to terminate the pregnancy as soon as possible. Our doctor encouraged me to carry the child to full term, but feeling the baby grow and kick for another month was more than I could bear. I needed to get through the delivery and get on with my life.

Note her preoccupation: *her* feelings, *her* life. The baby is now dismissed as a person. But here comes the surprising part.

Sometime during that night, as we went over and over what was happening to *us* [note again the preoccupation with her own life and feelings, not with what was happening to the *baby]* we began to think about all the appeals from the anguished parents of children awaiting liver, kidney, and heart transplants. . . . Maybe our baby's organs could give a sick child a chance to live. Maybe we could find something good in our tragic situation.

When we arrived at the hospital early the next morning, we were aggressive about out wish to donate our baby's organs.

Hospital staff pointed out that their child would not be legally "brain dead." The couple was also well aware that "once the brain stem stops, the organs give out, and it's too late for them to be useful."

Nonetheless, the law preventing people from carving up living babies "seemed so wrong." As Mrs. Marell put it, "How could anyone consider the quality of my daughter's short life above the life of a child who could have a chance? . . . It seems such a terrible *waste.* . . . The life cannot be saved. But that life could save others."

Here Mrs. Marell was being inaccurate. What she really meant was, "My daughter's *death* could save others." This, of course, is debatable, as transplants are no magic cure. People die right on the operating table while they are receiving transplants; they die afterwards from complications of the operation; they die from rejection of the organ; and so on. But the bottom line of the whole procedure is the hope of having your child's sacrifice benefit society. You, the adult sacrificing the child, want to feel better. As Mrs. Marell said, "The opportunity to have helped someone else through a difficult situation would certainly have eased my mind."[7]

We are supposed to be "sensitive" to the "anguish" felt by families such as these. This would be fine if these women and their husbands were not crusading to increase child sacrifice. Mrs. Marell, for instance, is trying to influence the California legislature to declare *all* anencephalic infants "dead" so that these helpless babies can be cut apart while living and their organs used for transplants.

Following her reasoning, it would be hard to see how *any* anencephalic baby could be allowed to die normally. If these babies' organs are *needed* and it would be a *waste* to not cut them up while alive to get at those organs, why should such sacrifice not be *compulsory?* Barbara Katz Rothman, a sociologist at Baruch College in New York, put her finger on this problem, saying, "There is a potential for making parents on all sides [both the parents of potential organ donors and the parents of children with serious organ problems] feel this is what *they ought to do.*" (emphasis ours)[8]

Thus, misguided "sensitivity" applied to those who actually appear remarkably insensitive ("I need to get on with my own life" is not exactly the cry of a motherly heart) allows them to promote death unhindered.

If you want to kill your baby, you shouldn't get applause for it.

Offending the Cultural Deities

You may have noticed the religious overtones of these mothers' desires to have their children sacrificed for organs. It is almost as if the parents (especially the mothers) are trying to atone for the social "sin" of having conceived a less-than-physically-perfect baby.

Wolf Wolfensberger speaks of "offending the cultural deities of youthfulness, beauty, fun, and escape from pain and suffering."[9]

Obviously, a handicapped child strongly offends these "deities." Perhaps less obvious is the strongly pagan thinking behind these court decisions that allow parents to decide to kill their children. As Wolfensberger perceptively notes:

> People should deeply contemplate the calamitous meaning of the 1980 Supreme Court decision regarding Philip Becker: rejecting and absentee parents may legally refuse life-sustaining medical procedures to be performed on their handicapped offspring, condemning a child to (a most likely slow and gruesome) death. We thus return to the concept of child-as-chattel who can be killed at the whim of the parent, *as was the case in pagan Greece and Rome* (emphasis ours).[10]

> The Supreme Court ruled that even absentee parents who had divested themselves of their handicapped child at birth may withhold permission for life-saving medical procedures for such a child despite the fact that their child with Down's Syndrome was rather capable. . . . [11]

We have already seen the connection between Nazism and New Age doctrine—of which this kind of court ruling is a blatant example. Now see how the Nazis, our leaders in these matters, went about placating the "cultural deities."

> The indications for killing eventually became wider and wider. Included were children who had "badly modeled ears," who were bed wetters, or who were perfectly healthy but designated as "difficult to educate." . . .
> A further method of "child euthanasia" was deliberately and literally starving children to death in the "children's divisions." . . .

Dr. Pfannmueller explained the routine. "We don't do it," he said, "with poisons or injections. Our method is much simpler and more natural." With these words, the fat and smiling doctor lifted an emaciated, whimpering child from his little bed, holding him up like a dead rabbit. He went on to explain that food is not withdrawn all at once, but rations are gradually decreased. "With this child," he added, "it will take another two or three days."[12]

How Do You Make a Dead Baby Float?

When the Sixties' generation were kids, there were joke fads. First came the elephant jokes, then the knock-knock jokes. Later came the gross-out make-your-mother-sick jokes: dead baby jokes. One that sticks in the memory of everyone who has heard it is the Dead Baby Float joke. It goes like this:

Q: How do you make a dead baby float?
A: A cup of soda water and two teaspoonfuls of dead baby.

That joke was never funny, and it's even less funny now, because babies are now actually being used as ingredients in jewelry, cosmetics, food, and medicine. This new cannibalism, exactly similar to the old pagan practices of using children for these very purposes, is unsqueamishly advertised as "medical progress" and faithfully reported as such by the media. Witness the following articles:

Using tissue from unborn infants to treat Parkinson's disease is a procedure that has been disclosed only in recent weeks. A Mexican doctor's letter to the *New England Journal of Medicine* reported substantial improvement in two patients who had received grafts of the material. A Philadelphia neurosurgeon later announced that he had performed similar transplants. The operations had occurred only since September.

At issue in the new procedure is whether the brain tissue and adrenal glands are taken from fetuses which were aborted or from those which miscarried. . . .

Also appearing on the program [*"Night Line"*] with the Mexican was a young woman *who volunteered to get pregnant and then to abort the child so that its tissues could be used* to treat her father, badly impaired by Parkinson's disease. Her father, however, insisted that he would never consider such a transplant. . . .

William Shuler Jr., a family practitioner in Mendota, Ill., wrote in the *Journal of Biblical Ethics in Medicine* last October: "It must be clearly understood and underlined that spontaneous abortions are not considered desirable for transplantation, because it is assumed that many of these fetuses may bear genetic defects which might well wreak havoc with the recipient in unexpected ways. *Precisely what is wanted is the normal, healthy preborn infant.*" [13]

Experiments with fetal tissue transplants already are being performed in Sweden. And Hana Biologics, a medical research company in Alameda, California, will begin experimental fetal tissue treatments this year in research hospitals. . . .

Other proponents of the new technology said that *knowing fetal tissue will help save a life can ease the inevitable pain a woman who has an abortion must feel.* . . .

Others wonder whether complex treatments demanding large amounts of fetal tissue to cure one individual of disease would create the need for large-scale "fetus farms" to meet the demand to transplant tissue in the medical marketplace. (emphasis ours in both quotes above)[14]

Kill Me, I'm Yours . . . It Will Make You Feel Better

Interesting, isn't it, that in both articles we find the idea advanced that abortion could become a noble gesture *if done for the purpose of providing baby's flesh* to be used for medical purposes? In this way, abortion moves from an offering to the god of Self (about which most women don't feel too good) to a genuinely religious New Age act. Children could be cannibalized "for the benefit of another person or society," just as in our definition of human sacrifice, and the parents would get to feel good about offering their own flesh and blood on the altar. In fact, just as in the old pagan religions, parents could be *coerced* or *forced* into offering their children for the sake of saving the life of some more "worthy" member of society.

Women already are picking up this kind of reasoning. "Atone for your sins by offering up your baby." The so-called surrogate mothers, who are actually the biological mothers of the children they give up, often appear to be "atoning" for the past in this way.

> One bizarre aspect about contemporary surrogate motherhood is that about a third of these women have either themselves had an abortion, or given up a baby for adoption . . . The link between the surrogate practice and deathmaking becomes also clearer when one considers that in many of these agreements, the surrogate mother promises to undergo amniocentesis and abortion if it appears that the child may be handicapped.[15]

But offering up your baby to another, more "worthy" woman is not enough for those who do not know Christ and have deeply insulted the "deities" by conceiving a defective child.

Picture the guilt, the shame that nonbelievers are made to feel in today's society when they bring a handicapped child into the world. This child is supposed to be a "drain on scarce resources," an "unproductive member of society," and so on. He or she also is most likely ugly by current Hollywood standards, and unable to take part in the youth-sex-and-health cult as well. The parents are told, through newspaper stories and TV reports, that they are "burdening society" with this child, and that conceiving and bearing him marks them as failures.

All this "sin" can be atoned for, and the parents can become heroes, if only they will *offer the child as a human sacrifice.*

Once the living baby is cut open and exploited as an organ or tissue bank, the parents have now accomplished something useful in society's eyes. Their formerly "worthless" child has become "productive"—even a lifesaver. The parents may, if they wish, get interviewed on TV and radio and see their pictures in the newspaper. They are feted as "ethical pioneers." Their sacrifice (actually, their *baby's* sacrifice) sets them apart as particularly selfless people blessed with an extra amount of sensitivity. Those lucky enough to get in on the ground floor of child sacrifice may even get book and movie contracts.

The baby, meanwhile, gets pain and death . . . exactly as in the old pagan religions.

They Said It

Are we being too hard on the parents who want to see their children used as organ farms?

See how they themselves describe what they are doing.

Dr. Timothy Frewen of University Hospital in London, Ontario, said that doctors had passed a "milestone" by using life-support equipment to benefit not the anencephalic baby but another who would receive her heart. He said in a telephone interview that he believed the strategy had opened the door to more widespread use of anencephalic babies as organ donors. And, he added, *it also gives some comfort to parents of lethally deformed infants because their child can "make a very significant contribution to life."* . . .

The parents of Baby Gabrielle insisted on *offering* her vital organs—saying they wanted their baby's short life to *have some value.*[16]

A couple want their fatally impaired child kept alive after birth long enough for its organs to be removed for transplants, but no hospital has agreed to the plan.

"This is a real tragedy because *these people want something good to come from their loss* and yes, we would like to help them out, said Dick Schaefer, a spokesman for Loma Linda, where many infant heart transplants have been performed.[17]

Baby Evelyn, a nine-day-old baby born with most of her brain missing, died while under the watch of the newborn intensive care staff at Loma Linda University Medical Center, spokeswoman Anita Rockwell said.

"She died peacefully," Rockwell said. "Her parents are saddened but *still are very pleased that their daughter could give some gift of life*" by making available her heart valves, eyes, and corneas for donation.[18]

In our two cases [the authors are doctors reporting on transplant operations using anencephalic babies are organ donors], both parents of the anencephalic fetuses expressed *relief of their suffering and mourning* when the option of donating the kidneys of their infants became available to them. . . . Harvesting the kidneys *helped the parents to see an additional moral purpose* in carrying the twin pregnancy for 20 weeks after the first diagnosis of anencephaly in one of the twins. In the other case . . . the possibility of organ transplantation, according to the parents' own words, *helped them to overcome their grief . . .*[19]

Brenda Winner has become a reluctant pioneer in medical ethics.
    She has won a battle for the right to have her doomed baby kept alive by machines so its [sic] organs can be donated to others. . .
    For Winner, *grief about losing her first child is eased by knowing that its organs will help others . . .*
    "I've been asked if I could actually cut up this baby, take the organs, and put them in another baby," she said. "My answer is, 'Yes, I could.'" (all above quotes, emphasis ours.)[20]

Could Child Sacrifice Become Compulsory?

The god of Mammon can also be expected to play a part in the coming wave of infant sacrifice, if we ever let things get that far. Already businessmen are drawing up price lists for baby parts. Bernard Nathanson, the now repentant co-founder of the National Abortion Rights Action League, told a group recently about a letter he had received from a counselor in his old abortion clinic.

She said she is still counseling in [abortion] clinics, she believes she is doing the right thing, but they've gone too far, she said. Now they are dickering over the sale of fetal tissue from these clinics to businessmen. She overheard a conversation in which they were actually drawing up the list of prices, with brain tissue, of course, at the highest price and arms and legs down at the bottom. This is not anecdotal; I have the letter to show you if you'd like.[21]

Even more ominously for those of us who have no intention of parting with our babies for money is the trend toward computerized genetic screening. California and Utah both now have centralized genetic records. Now Mammon, in the person of insurance companies, enters the door.

Insurance companies are considering the use of genetic tests to identify families who face a risk of an inherited disease or who may be generally susceptible to chronic diseases. . . .

In 1986, California became the first state to institute *mass prenatal screening*. . . . Pregnant women can refuse the test, but *they must sign a waiver of liability*. . . . Many medical experts believe the California program, if successful, could pave the way for mass prenatal screening in other states. . . .

Two years before Adolf Hitler enacted Nazi Germany's first "hereditary health law," at least 30 U.S. states had legislation that dealt, in some fashion, with "hereditary defectives," a category which included those with genetic diseases as well as drug addicts, drunkards and convicted criminals.

"Simplistic notions of human genetics have quite often proved to have political consequences," says Robert Cook-Deegan, a genetics expert at the congressional Office of Technology Assessment. . . .

Controlling inherited disease means *controlling the people who carry it*. Unlike infectious diseases, which may be caused by viruses or bacteria, a genetic disease cannot be isolated from the person it affects. . . .

"It is not out of the realm of possibility to use genetic testing, prenatal diagnosis and abortion as a means of reducing costs," says Dr. Neil Holtzman, an OTA expert in genetic testing. "If you have no means of treatment, it becomes *a very effective way to reduce costs*." . . .

Public health departments in the United States routinely screen infants for a number of inherited diseases. Until recently, the sole objective of state-imposed screening programs has been treatment of the affected infant—not the eradication of the disease.

Because the tests were always performed after birth, the question of testing was always separated from the issue of abortion. But *California now requires that every expectant mother be offered the test* to determine if her developing child suffers a neural tube defect, like spina bifida and anencephaly ... (emphasis ours)[22]

You don't need much imagination to see where these trends could take us.

(1) Compulsory genetic screening reveals your child will have a handicap.

(2) You are then told of your "duty" to offer the child as a medical sacrifice.

(3) Should you fail to comply, the state takes guardianship of your child in the womb and either
(a) forcibly aborts you (as in China) or
(b) takes your baby and forcibly sacrifices him or her.

(4) Force may not be necessary in most cases, because simply refusing medical coverage to such pregnancies would cause most people, lacking Christian principles, to go along with whatever will save their bank account—just as the Sierra Leone tribespeople went along with sacrificing their own children rather than risking their own lives and tribal status.

A Statue of Darwin in the Temple of Baal

We are not the only people to consider these possibilities. Writing in the *Journal of Biblical Ethics in Medicine*, physician William Shuler, Jr. painted this picture:

It could be easily argued that in our rush toward technological sophistication we have overshot even the most hardened pagans of ancient times, with hardly a blink from the never-sleeping eyes of the secular or religious media. I refer, of course, to our newly-discovered Saturnine capacity not only to kill tiny infants but to devour them as well. . . .

Cannibalism of children was always seen as a genuine and very severe, almost an ultimate, punishment, not a seductive element in any sense of the word. Many euphemisms will undoubtedly be developed for this fetal cell transplantation technology, but does it not merely amount to a rather sophisticated form of cannibalism? . . .

Let us suppose for a moment that applicability ascends rapidly [i.e., that these operations become more feasible and successful]; that abortion declines due to declining fertility, fear of AIDS, etc; and that Congress or the courts declare that a person's body is their own to sell, including all fetal tissue. In that scenario, the value of fetal parts might well exceed their weight in gold. And though it may stretch our imagination somewhat, it is not improbable that a form of "temple prostitution" will reassert itself in the temples of Molech. That is, certifiably healthy males and females could consent to reproduction solely for profit (the temple of Mammon) perhaps with a form of nature worship or biotechnical Darwinism thrown in (the temple of Baal).[23]

Time to Cleanse the Temple

We don't have to wonder what will happen to any nation that does such things—or to any church that fails to oppose them.

Look at Germany, the first modern New Age nation, now divided into two nations, one half under the heel of a heartless oppressor.

Look at Old Testament Israel and Judah.

Here are the reasons the Bible gives for the fall of Israel to the Assyrians, a people who dealt brutally with their captives.

All this took place because the Israelites had sinned against the Lord their God. . . . They worshiped other gods and followed the

practices of the nations the Lord had driven out before them. . . .
They did the things the Lord had forbidden them to do. . . . They
sacrificed their sons and daughters in the fire . . . so the Lord was
very angry with Israel and removed them from his presence. (2
Kings 17:7, 8,1 5, 18)

But we don't need to make their mistakes. The things that happened to the Israelites "were written down as warnings for us, on
whom the fulfillment of the ages has come" (1 Corinthians 10:11).
God knew about the New Age from the foundation of the world,
and he has not left us unprepared—if we are willing to listen.

"See, I set before you today life and prosperity, death and
destruction. For I command you today to love the Lord your God,
to walk in his ways, and to keep his commands, decrees, and
laws; then you will live and increase, and the Lord your God will
bless you in the land you are entering to possess" (Deuteronomy
30:15, 16).

PART IV: PREPPED FOR THE SACRIFICE

FOURTEEN

Terms of Surrender

Satan, the real master of the New Age, delights in mysterious code words and phrases because they allow his agents, when questioned, to escape public censure by hiding behind a verbal mirage. . . . Modern-day killers use such intentionally confusing terms as "neutralize," "waste," and "terminate with extreme prejudice" to indicate a person is about to be murdered. Hitler had his "final solution to the Jewish problem."

(Texe Marrs, *Dark Secrets of the New Age*)

The great masses of the people will more easily fall victim to a big lie than to a small one.

(Hitler)

The first thing to change when one [religion] overcomes another and takes over a society is language. When you control a people's way of describing things, you control their way of dealing with them.

(Dr. Robert Mendelsohn)

The tongue has the power of life and death .

(Proverbs 18:21)

Newspeak leads to Oldthink. The more we adopt the language of paganized science and medicine, the less we notice anything odd going on.

It's not that we have enthusiastically endorsed a revival of pagan sacrifice—actually, we haven't even noticed it. It all sounded so normal, so scientific, so up-to-date.

151

Dave Hunt and others have dealt with the way New Age thinking is creeping into the church through the use of loaded theological terms. In religion, we are being asked to think of man as god. The odd flip side of this is that, in things medical, we are being asked to think of man as dog. Thus, some of us become gods, and the rest become dogs to sacrifice to the gods.

Love Thy Vegetable as Thyself?

God gave us *two* great commands: the first, to love the Lord our God with our whole heart and soul and mind and strength, and the second, "like unto it," to love our neighbor as ourselves.

It is not enough to reject pagan thinking in our doctrine of God; we must also refuse to accept it in our doctrine of man.

Today, media and medical terms directly insult the doctrine of man as created in the image of God. We hear people called:

- vegetables
- monsters
- organisms
- uncooperative elements
- neo-morts
- members of our species
- lower consciousnesses
- retardates
- anencephalics
- terminal cases
- idiots
- brain dead
- fetuses
- defectives
- irreversibles
- "it"
- gomers (compassionate medical slang for "Get Out Of My Emergency Room")

Now, try plugging one of those terms into this sentence: "Love thy —— as thyself." Love thy neo-mort as thyself? Thy fetus as thyself? Thy vegetable as thyself? "It" as thyself? The very use of these words makes Christian love seem ridiculous, if not impossible. In each case, a person ends up sounding like a bit of damaged goods from the supermarket, or a bit of matter with no more feelings than a rock.

These names for people are *terms of surrender*. To use them is to surrender to a pagan consciousness that sees people as commodities, consumable by the gods. The real revival of paganism starts right here. As the Bible says, "The tongue has the power of life and death," meaning you can condemn someone to death or bless him with life simply by *what you choose to call him*.

Margaret's Choice: "The Path to Earthly Paradise" Is Paved with the Bodies of Human Weeds

The pioneer of "people-as-lower-consciousnesses" in America was Margaret Sanger, the founder of Planned Parenthood. She was the first to loudly and successfully promote the idea that some people are "human weeds." Sanger followed this up with suggestions for how to rid ourselves of the "weeds."

Sanger reasoned as follows:

(1) The weeds breed too much. Therefore, the "mentally and physically fit" ought to breed more in an attempt to outbreed the weeds.

(2) Since the superior classes refuse to do this, the next step is to forcibly sterilize the weeds wherever possible, and offer birth control and abortion where it is not.

(3) For more immediate results, withdraw all forms of charity and life-support from the weeds. Sanger put it this way:

As a matter of sober fact, the benevolent activities of our missionary societies to reduce the death-rate by prevention of infanticide and checking of disease, actually serve in the end to aggravate the pressure of population upon its food-supply and to increase the severity of the inevitably resultant catastrophe.[1]

The actual dangers can only be fully realized when we have acquired definite information concerning the financial and cultural cost of these classes to the community, when we become fully cognizant of the burden of the imbecile upon the whole human race; when we see the funds that should be available for human development, for scientific, artistic and philosophic research, being diverted annually, by hundreds of millions of dollars, to care and segregation of men, women and children who should never have been born.[2]

(4) Benefit to society of all the above: cost-savings and a higher quality environment (no more ugly and stupid people around to bother her).

To promote her agenda, Sanger relied heavily on insulting language. In just one sentence, for example, she spoke of "the inferior classes . . . the feeble-minded, the mentally defective, the poverty stricken . . . "[3] She also, foreshadowing the state of things to come, spoke approvingly of "conditions of life among the primitive tribes" that prevented "the unhealthy growth of sentimentality."[4]

Sanger was actively hostile, not only to the "feeble-minded" and other "weeds," but to Biblical Christianity.

I have touched upon these various aspects of the complex problem of the feeble-minded, and the menace of the moron to human society, not merely for the purpose of reiterating that it is one of the greatest and most difficult problems of modern times, demanding an immediate, stern and definite policy, but because it illustrates the *actual harvest of reliance on traditional morality,* upon the *biblical injunction to increase and multiply.* (emphasis ours)[5]

Sanger went even farther than this. She explicitly denied the doctrine (she called it the "illusion") of Heaven[6] and called sex the "radiant force" that would enable mankind to attain "the great spiritual illumination which will transform the world, which will light up the only path to an earthly paradise."[7] The means to this end sound astonishingly like modern New Age teaching: "by knowing ourselves, by expressing ourselves, by realizing ourselves more completely than has ever before been possible . . . we shall attain the kingdom."[8] No wonder she approvingly quoted Sir Francis Galton, the British scientist who wanted to introduce Eugenics "into the national conscience like a new religion" and stated that she saw "no impossibility in Eugenics becoming religious dogma among mankind."[9]

From Weeds to Resources

Margaret Sanger, however, did not go so far as to call people *resources.* She wanted to get rid of some of us; she didn't think of cannibalizing us. That explains why Planned Parenthood, officially at least, still resists the use of aborted babies' bodies for experiments, even though it continues to actively hustle millions of abortion deaths per year.

Here, big business and our own government have led the way. Personnel departments have been renamed "Departments of Human Resources." Numerous states (usually those with the most anti-family policies) have "Divisions of Human Resources." Governors give speeches labeling children "our greatest resource."

Resources, obviously, are made to be *used,* and it didn't take long before the push was on to exploit people who "aren't any good for anything else." Now, for example, the transplant debate, such as it is, centers around who is brain dead when, and not whether it is OK to use people (alive or dead) as a tissue resource. Increasingly we hear about how "wasteful" it is not to exploit aborted babies as medicine for Parkinson's sufferers, and what a "misuse of resources" it would be to allow healthy, though defective, people to keep hanging on to their own organs.

This is precisely the line of reasoning the Nazis (who also had New Age leanings) took. They had been prepped for human sacrifice by the writings of a judge and a psychiatrist, Karl Binding and Albert Hoche. Well before the Nazi era, Binding and Hoche were complaining about "The tremendous care that these creatures receive; creatures of no value at all, indeed who are quite an obstacle."[10] Binding and Hoche spoke of "ballast-type persons of no value."[11]

Just like Margaret Sanger, Binding and Hoche raised the issue of people as weeds. It remained for the Nazis to discover *uses* for the "ballast-type persons"—and for modern medicine to improve on the Nazis.

From Resources to Victims

The simple inhumanity of looking at people as "resources" can lead to more ominous developments. Legislators may talk about children as resources in order to drum up more funding for state education, but they are not thinking of *using* the children in the same way we use farm animals or heavy machinery. Not at first, anyway. But once the idea that people are resources is fully accepted, the logical question arises: Resources for what?

We are talking about unholy sacrifices, remember. In order to have a sacrifice you must have a victim. If each person is a human being made in the image of God and possessing a spirit and soul, then obviously no one person can be sacrificed for the sake of another against his consent. But if some people—or all of us—become "resources," then what?

Consider how far we have already come. First, humanism stripped life of its religious value. The only value left was evolutionary utilitarianism, which is a fancy way of saying "The benefit of society as our leaders see it." Next, certain classes of people became nonpersons. At this point, your future prospects already look dim if someone can prove that your death would bring an emotional, financial, or medical benefit to someone else. Still, provided that you yourself are healthy and somehow contributing to society, you are not a likely candidate for sacrifice, since evolutionists worship the healthy, beautiful, and productive. This was the first surge of the New Wave in medicine.

Now, the New Age comes along with a *new* religion to fill up the empty holes humanism left, a *new* utilitarianism, and a *new* ethic of sacrifice. What if your suffering can be shown to have a *spiritual* benefit for others—such as appeasing the angry Earth Goddess who has been defiled by pollution? What if, instead of humanists' insistence that aborted babies and other victims "feel no pain," we discover that pain is an illusion that can safely be ignored—even when the victim is screaming and thrashing about? What if sacrificing your near and dear turns out to be not only beneficial to you, but a *noble* and *necessary* sacrifice on your part? What if sacrifice turns out to be *good* for the victim—improving his or her karma and providing a better life in the next reincarnation?

We already have our sacrifices. Abortions—millions of them. Comatose people deprived of food and water. More gruesome practices than these, even, are becoming commonplace. However, so far someone has to consent before a person can be killed for another person's benefit. Now imagine what could happen if *nobody* needed to consent to a sacrifice, except some priest-like figure who ordered it? What if the sacrifice did not need to benefit *anybody?*

New Labels for Old Sacrifices

How far can language be distorted to convince us of the need for innocent deaths? Farther than you might think. For example, most laymen would hardly suspect when we hear "heart transplant," that what we are really talking about is that "the beating heart of a living person was cut out of him, resulting in his death, and it (the heart) was given to and used by another person whose life was deemed more valuable than the original user of the heart."

Who knows when journalists write about "pulling the plug" that they could mean "stop feeding through the tube so that the person dies in agony over days or weeks from thirst or starvation" or "the ventilator (or respirator) is removed so that his weak lungs, unable to lift the weight of his ribs, desperately seek for air and he suffocates from his own disability"? "Pull the plug" is such a convenient word-picture, reminding us of pulling the plug on the table lamp. The light "dies" instantly and painlessly. The patient whose plug is pulled, unfortunately, does not.

We regularly hear people referred to as "vegetables" (not speaking) or "biologically tenacious" (it's hard to kill them). They are said to be "not there" even when interviews with formerly comatose people confirm that many can hear and are aware of what is happening around them.

Even the legitimate word *patient* is being used as a tool to distance doctors and nurses, and even family, from the humanity of the sick. These words do matter. As one speaker noted:

> "Defective implies the legal right to reject. We also do a grave injustice to ourselves, the parents, and the baby when we label the child as 'it.' It's a cop out by categorizing the baby as non-human. We do the labeling in an attempt to make it less painful if the decision is made not to treat the child."[12]

Quality of Life

"Quality of life," perhaps the most potent weapon in the New Wave language arsenal, started its now checkered career as a phrase referring to external conditions which added to or detracted from the quality of one's life. Life itself was never in question; only its quality would be improved. Now "quality of life" has been gutted and stuffed with a new meaning; a new meaning not designed to improve the conditions of people's lives, but tailored to facilitate the taking of lives of "poor quality." Instead of *removing poor conditions to improve lives,* we are asked to *remove poor lives to improve conditions.*

When writers and speakers talk about about "quality of life," few of them could tell you the criteria by which this judgement would be made. They have no idea that they too are being measured, nor would they know how to measure up. But "quality of life" sounds so compassionate, so well-thought-out. Great medical minds talk about it. Surely we wouldn't want to use "extraordinary means" (read: food and water) to "artificially prolong " (save) the life of people who would be "useless" (inconvenient) or a "burden" (expensive) to their families and society (costing us something in taxes or insurance).

Death by the Numbers

> It is no good saying that the words you use don't matter.
> They matter immensely. Try to imagine a world where
> people are addressed only by their numbers. (William
> Kirk Kilpatrick)[13]

In one study, six of seven doctors interviewed were "in agreement that some selective nontreatment of defective neonates is necessary."[14]

Selective nontreatment, in plain English, means being neglected to death; neglecting your food, water, warmth . . . whatever is keeping you alive. The term "neonates" in this context sounds suspiciously and ominously like "neo-morts" mentioned earlier in this book. Once we accept the idea of selective nontreatment of handicapped babies, is there any reason why doctors would refuse to "selectively nontreat" *any* "defective" person?

Again, the emerging sacrificial process was covered up by scientific-sounding terms. In this case, a *formula* with *numbers* that doctors and others could plug in was the engine for a new wave of sacrifice.

As early as 1942, American doctor Foster Kennedy recommended that a Stanford I.Q. test be used to measure retarded children and that those below a certain mark be killed and that those above that point be sterilized and trained for work because, as he said, " . . . they are greatly needed for the simpler forms of work. They are necessary for the work of the world."[15]

A more precise equation for who should live and who should die was determined by the Oklahoma Experiment. After observations of sixty-nine infants with spina bifida, some receiving "vigorous treatment," and others receiving only "supportive care" (no treatment), some medical leaders concluded that life or death decisions could and should be made on the basis of the formula $QL=NE(H+S)$.

The formula sounds mathematically precise, as indeed it was intended to sound. But not only is it intrinsically anti-biblical, it is extremely easy to manipulate by anyone with a vested interest in another person's death.

$QL=NE(H+S)$

"In this formula, QL=NE(H+S), QL is quality of life, NE represents the patient's natural endowments, both physical and intellectual, H is the contribution from the home and family, and S is the contribution from society."[16]

Note that the doctors call the people they are assessing "patients." Again, this loaded term implies that the doctors intend to help, when they actually intend to decide *if* the "patient" shall be helped. The decision itself is made on the basis of the patient's prophesied future quality of life.

Note also that it is always others who actually decide the "quality" of the life that the potential patient is living. The breakthrough here is the fact that someone has finally decided to list the components of what would be a "quality" life. The "equals" sign gives us permission to closely examine if there is indeed "equality" on both sides of the equation.

Actually, nobody is able to determine if someone else's life has that intangible substance, quality, in the first place. Many people ignorantly agree with quality of life assessments because they think of how they would feel should they suddenly find themselves in the same condition as the person who's being judged. This completely ignores how the handicapped individual actually feels having lived with this condition throughout his life, or the tenacity of the human spirit when faced with new challenges.

Do the handicapped *want* to die? If it were so, suicide would be rampant among the mentally retarded, terminal, deformed, and handicapped people. Yet these people have a suicide rate *lower* than the general population. By that reasoning, college students, and medical students in particular, who commit suicide at proportionately higher rates, must be the ones who feel that their lives do not have "quality"!

Now we come to the actual definition, the first part being "natural endowments," NE for short. These NE are divided into categories of physical and intellectual. The immediate fallacy of this is that it may be impossible to neatly separate these two because of their interdependence. An example that comes readily to mind is that of Helen Keller and her multiple disabilities: deafness, blindness, and muteness (by way of her deafness). No test in the world, then or now, would be effective in discovering her intellect, which was considerable, because she was physically unable to understand or respond.

We are only now beginning to chart the depths of the human mind. How can we presume, in the infancy of our study, to determine whether or not someone is thinking in there just because *we* cannot communicate with *him?*

The idea of determining a person's life or death based on his shape, inside or out, is completely un-Christian. Furthermore, both physical and intellectual evaluations are quite capable of change over the course of a lifetime. A scar here, an accident there and a person could end up *looking* quite inhuman—but judging him thereby would *be* inhuman. Mental capacities can change for all sorts of reasons over the years. Will someone next suggest periodic tests so that no "neo-defects" drain our resources?

The factor of NE is then multiplied by a small equation of the available resources of home added to those of society. Both of these elements require an ability to prophesy that would be the envy of every psychic known to the *National Enquirer.* Will these "concerned" individuals interview every member of the family, extracting dollar amounts and time schedules that each is willing to "pledge"? Is there any accounting of the fact that disabled children are not usually abandoned, and that most families with them (media publicity geared to the anti-child exceptions to the contrary) are not continually grumbling about "burdens" but seem to be actually happy? There are even people who adopt *only* disabled children. Will these prophecies of the availability of caring family members be made on the basis of tea leaves . . . chicken entrails?

Nothing limits these evaluations to any particular age. If we accept this criterion, we must accept it for all people, including ourselves . . . even if we initially think that it is limited to handicapped infants and sick old people. A warning:

"Be not deceived; God is not mocked: for whatsoever a man soweth, that shall he also reap"(Galatians 6:7 KJV).

And this is not karma, where you get back what you put in, but sowing and reaping where you get back *bushels* of what you put in.

Sacrifice of the Unfittest

The treatment-by-death mentality is by no means limited to those who appear to be dying. We can see a lot about what is being planned for our future by the way the word "unfit" is creeping into medical discussions.

"Unfit" means something a lot worse than "disabled" or "handicapped." "Unfit" people not only have problems, but *do not deserve to have their problems treated*. They are misfits, people who should not even be alive—that is what the word "unfit" *means*. So do words like "non-human," "dead," "better-off-dead," or "miserable life."

Does God give the gift of life to "unfit" people? Since we live in an imperfect world, all of us are imperfect physically or mentally to some degree or other. Our imperfections, however, do not make us inhuman. Humanity is a matter of the spirit that the Bible says dwells not in our brain but in our hearts.

Handicapped people have shown repeatedly that their limitations do not limit but challenge them. But even were this not so, their lives would be worth protecting, if only for the sake of maintaining *our own* humanity.

Leave On the Mr. Yuck Labels

> Making immoral action look neat is now sometimes termed detoxification. (Wolf Wolfensberger)[17]

Is it loving to label the poison bottle "candy" and leave it where the children can reach it? Absolutely not! That is why so many manufacturers of dangerous substances take pains to label their product with green "Mr. Yuck" faces, so children will know enough to leave them alone.

Christians can do the same with language. But if we use these detoxified terms—unfit, vegetable, terminal, and so on—it's like ripping off the Mr. Yuck labels and relabeling death as candy.

Shine the Light and Sound the Trumpet

Scripture warns us against "perverse" speech and lips. This is not primarily an injunction against foul language or dirty jokes, but against *twisted words,* words with false meaning which are calculated to deceive.

We don't have to use these terms of death; we can *re-toxify* the language (as Dr. Wolfensberger might have it). Honest words such as "starvation" and "thirst torture" can take the place of phrases calculated to deceive, such as "omit treatment to permit a terminally ill patient whose death is imminent to die" (from the AMA statement on why it's now OK to deprive helpless people of food and water). Humane words such as "person," "man," "woman," "old lady," "baby," and "helpless human being" can replace death-making insults such as "vegetative" and "terminal." Using the right words, and not backing down, *will* make a difference.

If you are concerned about the tremendous advantage—media influence, government connections, and so on—that New Wave forces have gained, and feel like simply changing our personal use of words can't matter, remember the story of Gideon.

Gideon and his three hundred men, armed only with torches and trumpets, routed the huge Midianite army. This is how they did it. When Gideon gave the signal, he and his men, who had arranged themselves on the hills surrounding the Midianites, broke the pitchers to let the lights shine, blew on their trumpets, and shouted, "The sword of the Lord and of Gideon!" The Lord Himself then took a hand, throwing the entire Midianite army into confusion. The Midianites turned on each other, then fled in wild disarray. At this, the neighboring Israelites finally found their courage and pursued and wiped out the Midianites (Judges 7).

Honest words are like light on a dark subject, and fearless declaration of God's truth is like sounding a trumpet. We can take back more ground than we think simply by switching from pagan "terms of surrender" to honest Scriptural language—and by saying the truth *loudly.*

"So do not be afraid of them. There is nothing concealed that will not be disclosed, or hidden that will not be made known. What I tell you in the dark, speak in the daylight; what is whispered in your ear, proclaim from the housetops." (Jesus, speaking in Matthew 10:27)

If we are Christians, let's start talking like Christians. Let's start saying, "Thus saith the Lord," and "This is what the Bible says," instead of hiding our light under a pluralistic, secular bushel basket. Let's act *proud* of our Lord and of His Word! That is the way to begin turning this society from paganism back to Jesus Christ.

FIFTEEN

Idols in White Coats

*When a new religion wants to discredit an old religion,
it does so by blaming the problems of the people on the
old gods. Modern Medicine says your disease is caused
by a virus. Who created the virus? The old God. And so
on. . . .*

*Modern Medicine can give you a new God that can
counteract all the pesky forms of life that get in the way,
such as bacteria, viruses, cells dividing out of control,
inconvenient fetuses, deformed or retarded children, and
old people. . .*

The God of Modern Medicine is death

(Dr. Robert Mendelsohn)

Little children, keep yourselves from idols. (1 John 5:21)

C all her "S." For legal reasons, she does not
want to be identified.

S. has a grandmother who last year was
admitted to a Minneapolis hospital.

S. and her grandmother are the witnesses. Here is their story:

"Grandma's roommate, who was in her late eighties, was
there first. She had fallen and broken her hip; her daughter flew in
from the East.

"The daughter explained to 'S' that her mother would never
walk again and would spend the rest of her life in a wheelchair.
Until the accident, the older lady had lived in her own apartment,
but now she would have to go to a nursing home, an unsatisfactory
solution.

"Evidently the daughter, who said she had been concerned about her mother's ability to live alone before, found the thought of a wheelchair overwhelming. Anxious to go home, she requested that all food and fluids be removed so that her mother could die. While her mother was still in the hospital, she held an estate sale.

"'S' told me that the woman called out, over and over, 'Water . . . water . . . water.' Her voice was strong enough to carry to Grandma's bedside, across the room. It appeared to 'S' that the woman was miserable. Nurses would come in and swab her mouth, but she still cried for water. . . . After six days, the woman died."[1]

ᴈ   ᴈ   ᴈ   ᴈ   ᴈ

Now let us consider this tale of modern medical care from a slightly different angle.

Suppose that the little old lady in Grandma's room had been kidnapped by criminals instead of brought to a hospital.

Suppose that the kidnappers had thrown her roughly into the back of their shack and left her there without food and water until she died of thirst and starvation.

Suppose they had heard her pleading for water and ignored her.

Suppose that while the little old lady was tied up in the back of their shack the kidnappers had returned to her home, stripped it of valuables, and sold the valuables.

What would the press have said *then?*

"Little Old Lady Tortured to Death by Pitiless Kidnappers" is one likely headline. So is "Old Woman Dies of Thirst While Kidnappers Hold Sale."

Now suppose that the kidnappers had done their vile acts while in the pay of the little old lady's daughter. We could then expect headline like "Daughter Held Sale While Mom Cried for Water." Prosecuting attorneys and policemen would be doing their utmost to have such a woman and her henchmen sentenced to the maximum extent of the law.

But because this crime occurred in a *hospital* . . . because *nurses* and *doctors* were the ones torturing a little old woman to death, in spite of her cries for help . . . there was no public outrage. Even after an article carrying the details of the case appeared in a major newspaper, nothing was done.

The Sacred Rite

Some may think we have gone too far in this book, trying to establish the link between new medical trends and ancient pagan sacrifice. Actually, we have not gone far enough.

Let us now make the connection explicit.

As Nigel Davies informs us in *Human Sacrifice in History and Today,* "Ritual and religion are inseparable from human sacrifice; indeed, we may define the term as killing with a spiritual or religious motivation, usually, but not exclusively, accompanied by ritual."[2]

In the little old lady's case, the "ritual" was that of nurses checking her occasionally and even swabbing her mouth—thus giving the *appearance* of medical care while brutally denying her the real thing. Part of the sacred rite was performed by her daughter ritually signing her over to slow, tortuous death—just as relatives frequently offered their own flesh and blood to the gods of the past.

The Sacred Site

Davies continues, "Normally it was performed in a sacred place or one that had been made sacred for the occasion . . ."[3] In this case, the mere fact that the crime was perpetrated in a *hospital* made its performance above suspicion. If that helpless old woman had been treated that way anywhere except a hospital by anyone except medical people, her death would have been considered a particularly horrible murder. Because it occurred in the sacred site, it took on a completely different meaning—a socially acceptable meaning—even though the results for her were exactly the same as if she had died the victim of kidnappers in a lonely shack or hotel room, or if her daughter had tied her up and starved her to death in a closet of her own house.

The Sacred Idol

Now we come to the heart of the matter.

What makes the sacred site sacred?

It is because the idol sanctifies the sacred site.

Without going any farther, it is obvious that some strange god *must* be worshiped in hospitals where such brutal ritual murder can take place without attracting public concern. Otherwise, why this peculiar apathy about behavior that would arouse public ire if performed anywhere else?

Writing at a time when medical ethics had not even degenerated as far as they have today, internationally famous pediatrician Robert Mendelsohn made the bold claim, "Modern Medicine can't survive without our faith, because Modern Medicine in neither an art nor a science. *It's a religion*" (emphasis ours).[4] Dr. Mendelsohn went on to say, "Doctors are really the priests of the Church of Modern Medicine."[5]

What did Dr. Mendelsohn mean by calling Modern Medicine a religion? He was not referring to real medical advances like antibiotics (properly used) or better hygiene. Nor was he referring to those medical practitioners who are still struggling to hold the line of the old ethic, serving their patients and fighting for health and life. He meant the same thing we mean when we talk about paganized medicine—the cult of Death—because according to Mendelsohn, "The God of Modern Medicine is death."[6]

Why would a respectable, eminent pediatrician say a thing like that? And the late Dr. Mendelsohn (he just died in April 1988) *was* an eminent pediatrician. He served as Chairman of the Medical Licensing Committee for the State of Illinois; was Associate Professor of Preventive Medicine and Community Health in the School of Medicine of the University of Illinois; and was National Director of Project Head Start's Medical Consultation Service. He received numerous awards for his medical work and was widely in demand as a speaker on medical issues. Why would such a man, honored by the very medical establishment itself, write a book called *Confessions of a Medical Heretic* (Contemporary Books, 1979) in which he lambastes modern medicine as an idolatrous religion?

Mendelsohn calls Modern Medicine "idolatrous" because "what it holds sacred are not living things but mechanical processes. It doesn't boast of saving souls or lives but of how many times this or that new machine was used and how much money was taken in by the process."[7] He calls it a "religion" because its devotees (meaning us, the general population) have learned to take what Modern Medicine does *on faith*. If a *doctor* does it, it's OK. If a *bio-ethicist* labels it ethical, it is. If a *hospital* supervises it, it's medical care—even if the "care" is actually long, lingering, unnecessary *death*.

Mendelsohn points out the trend towards pagan sacrifice:

> We just can't get away from the fact that a disturbing amount of doctors' energies are devoted to death-oriented activities. I tell my students that to succeed in Modern Medicine all you have to do is look for some field that encourages death or thinking about death and you've got a brilliant future ahead of you. As far as Modern Medicine is concerned, death is a growth industry. You can't pick up a medical journal without reading the latest on: contraception, abortion, sterilization, genetic counseling and screening, amniocentesis, zero population growth, "death with dignity," "quality of life," and euthanasia. All of these activities have as their purpose the prevention of or termination of life. . . .
>
> In our rush to embrace these activities—with enthusiasm I can only describe as religious fervor—we are duped into both ignoring their dehumanizing effects and their lack of scientific justification. They are sacraments, after all. Sacraments of death.[8]

Doctors Now Kill More People Than They Help

Does this heading surprise you? It did us, the first time we saw it.

Yet it is true.

Doctors really do now kill more people than they help to heal.

We are so conditioned to think of modern medicine as a "healing" ministry that we don't realize doctors are the biggest death-dealers in the modern world. With over 20,000,000 legal abortions annually worldwide—all performed by doctors—modern medicine would have to be tremendously adept at lifesaving just to counter this immense amount of human sacrifice. Add to this the people like "S's" grandma's roommate put to death or neglected to death in hospitals and nursing homes (a number Wolf Wolfensberger estimates at 200,000 annually in the USA alone), and you're looking at an almost unparalleled holocaust. And, as we have seen, the new priests are not satisfied even with that. They are now pushing to declare anencephalic babies "brain absent" (another 3,000 victims per year in the USA), to withhold spoon-feeding from Altzheimer's sufferers (a number in the millions), to use all the medically dependent as organ donors (more millions), and so on. As Mendelsohn noted back in 1979,

> Modern Medicine is now better geared for killing people than it is for healing them. You see this best at both ends of life, where life is more delicate and death is closer and easier to ascribe to "natural causes." It's becoming increasingly dangerous, for instance, for a Mongoloid newborn with an intestinal obstruction to reside in a nursery. Though the obstruction is surgically correctable, there is an increasing likelihood that he will be deprived of care and allowed to [actually, forced to] die. The same goes for retarded children in state hospitals who are unfortunate enough to fall seriously ill.
>
> At the other end of life, "undesirables" are allowed or even encouraged to die. Old people in nursing homes, despite the flowery advertisements accompanying those places, are put there to keep them out of "real" people's way. They're put there to die, and they generally take the hint. . . .
>
> In cultures not yet under the death swoon of Modern Medicine, people live to advanced age in full possession of their capacities. But Modern Medicine renders old people *incapable* [often through drugs and gloomy prognostication].[9]

In view of all this, we are perfectly justified in calling New Wave doctors not just priests, but idols.

Idols of the New Age?
Parents would not simply chop up their anencephalic baby and throw her in the garbage. Neither would they hand their living

baby over to a plumber, or truck driver, or computer programmer, and say, "Cut her open." But they *would* offer her up . . . to the transplant surgeon.

Courts would not hand little old ladies over to secretaries, or gardeners, or mailmen, with total license to abuse the little old ladies to death. But they *do* hand them over . . . to nursing homes and hospitals.

When the living are handed over to New Wave doctors to be made into the dead, those handing the living over feel *good* about what they have done. We have already quoted numerous parents of anencephalic babies to show that offering these children to doctors makes the parents feel *better*. Similarly, "easing social tension," which Nigel Davies says is one of the two great purposes of human sacrifice,[10] is blissfully accomplished when the economically burdensome victim is ceremonially done to death by the proper people (medical people) in the sacred place (a medical facility). This relieving of social tension is also accomplished when "useless" people are sanctified by being offered up to the medical researcher. We have given many instances of this already: here is one more, from the many examples Dr. Mendelsohn personally witnessed decades ago.

> Surgery can be put to many uses besides the stated purpose of correcting or removing a disease process. Surgery is a great teaching tool as well as a fertile experimental field—although the only thing that's ever "learned" or "discovered" is how to perform the surgery. When I was Senior Pediatric Consultant to the Department of Mental Health in Illinois, I cut out a certain kind of operation that was being performed on mongoloid children with heart defects. The stated purpose of the operation was to improve oxygen supply to the brain. The real purpose, of course, was to improve the state's residency program in cardiovascular surgery, because nothing beneficial happened to the brains of mongoloid children—and the surgeons knew that. The whole idea was absurd. And deadly, since the operation had a fairly high mortality rate. Naturally, the university people were very upset when I cut out the operation. They couldn't figure out a better use for the mongoloid children.[11]

Doctors are not the only ones to blame for these deathward trends. We must also consider those who are *creating* the "social tensions" that lead to a demand for ritual sacrifice. Journalists. Judges. Lawyers. Professors. Social service workers. Psychologists. In short, the *experts*—those who claim superior wisdom, knowledge, and power—just as the pagan gods always claimed superior wisdom, knowledge, and power.

These are the people who are destroying our compassion for the feeble and vulnerable—who are always talking about costs versus benefits and scarce resources—who are planting the "us" versus "them" mind-set in our generation. They phrase the questions—like "Should we spend scarce funds on keeping the terminal elderly alive, *or* use it for educating the young . . . or public parks . . . or lower taxes?" They then "research" the answers—in the process educating the public—and present this research as reasons for moving towards more unholy sacrifice. They then *enforce* the sacrifices (if they are the New Jersey Supreme Court or the U.S. Supreme Court) and *preach* the sacrifices (if they are journalists, writers, or speakers). They get away with it because the word of these people is considered *superior* to any revealed religious code—particularly the Bible.

This has all been done before . . . recently, in fact. You don't have to go back to ancient Babylon to find the exact same order of events and the exact same people running the show. Just go back to New Age-stricken Nazi Germany and you will find a sinister trail leading directly to our own backyard.

SIXTEEN

Knives of Steel, Hearts of Marble, Feet of Clay

Whether to kill the Jews: an ethical dilemma. *Obviously, whether to kill Jews is an ethical dilemma only to those who are already inclined to kill them, such as perhaps the Nazis. But we can easily see how the framing of a situation can predispose people's minds in a morally false direction. This is exactly what happened in a very large headline in the* **Toronto Globe and Mail** *of July 18, 1987: "Brain Absent Babies Pose Transplant Dilemma." In other words, if so-called anencephalic babies would just quit appearing, they would not present us with the dilemma of whether to kill them for the sake of their organs.* (Wolf Wolfensberger)[1]

It was an attempt by a disciple, but it did not work.
(New Age theosophist Foster Bailey, most likely referring to Hitler's attempt at world dominion)[2]

Do not call conspiracy
    everything that these people call conspiracy;
do not fear what they fear,
    and do not dread it.
The Lord Almighty is the one you are to regard as holy,
    he is the one you are to fear,
    he is the one you are to dread,
and he will be a sanctuary . . . (Isaiah 8:12-14)

I dolatry is not just bowing down in front of carved images. If that were all there was to idolatry, the nations of the past would not have been foolish enough to do it.

Idolatry, in essence, is worship of evil spirits. The idols are just the symbols of the real gods: Sex, Pleasure, Money, Health, Youth, Power. Worshipers show their faith by doing whatever the gods require without question—even to the extent of unholy sacrifice.

When Christians stop questioning earthly authorities, and accept their teachings and rulings without examining them in the light of the Bible, we become idolaters. *Any* group of people, or person, who we are willing to follow blindly and cannot bear to consider fallible is an idol. When he appears, the Antichrist will be the ultimate idol—but in the meantime God has warned us to be wary because "even now many antichrists have come" (1 John 2:18).

Many Antichrists Have Come

Many antichrists *have* come. They briefly came to power in Nazi Germany, and have now spread like a cancer throughout all Western nations. This is the modern cult of experts who come "in their own names" and demand that we obey them because they (like the old gods) know best.

Inevitably, the new gods demand human sacrifices—more and more of them. An example is the way children were systematically slaughtered in Nazi Germany.

> The indications for killing eventually became wider and wider. Included were children who had "badly modeled ears," who were bed wetters, or who were perfectly healthy but designated as "difficult to educate."[3]

"Ah, that was just the Nazis!" we tend to think. "There are no Nazis in America today . . . except for some tiny sects of white supremacists, who the media and the police ruthlessly pursue the minute they show their heads."

Did you know that the Nazis were *not* the originators of the German Holocaust? The Nazis just added the Jews to a long list of people *already* slated for slaughter.

The real force behind the Holocaust was . . . well, let Dr. Frederic Wertham, a man who extensively studied the Holocaust and who wrote the definitive book on the German euthanasia program, tell us. (The emphasis in the following quotes is ours.)

> From its very inception the "euthanasia" program was guided in all important matters, including concrete details, by psychiatrists. . . .
>
> It has been stated that the psychiatrists were merely following a law or were being forced to obey an order. . . . The tragedy is that *the psychiatrists did not have an order. They acted on their own.* They were not carrying out a death sentence pronounced by somebody else. They were the legislators who laid down the rules for deciding who was to die. . . .
>
> In July, 1939, several months before Hitler's note was written, a conference took place in Berlin in which the program to kill mental patients in the whole of Germany was outlined in concrete, final form. . . .
>
> What psychiatrists did made even members of the Nazi Party weep.[4]

> *The backbone of the whole project was the experts.* It was their decision which sealed the fate of every victim . . . These experts were not new appointees of the Nazi regime, but had long and honorable careers. They were by no means products of Nazism. . . . Most of them had all the hallmarks of civic and scientific respectability. They were not Nazi puppets, but had made their careers and reputations as psychiatrists long before Hitler came to power. . . . They are still quoted in international psychiatric literature, which testifies to their scientific stature.[5]

Wertham's book, *The German Euthanasia Program*, makes two main points.

(1) The Holocaust was not forced on the experts. They designed and ran it.

(2) Our own New Wave expert leadership in America today has been trained by disciples of the Nazi era experts, using the accounts of Nazi human sacrifices as source material.

Trained by the Nazis, At Large in the USA

Wolf Wolfensberger, in a scholarly article entitled "The Extermination of Handicapped People in World War II Germany," shows how even during the Nazi era American experts were calling for compulsory child sacrifice—and after the Nazis were defeated, these experts kept on using Nazi ideas and literature in their own educational institutions.

> The euthanasia program originated in Germany within the culture of medicine, modern intellectualism, academicism, and scientism. The program began not because it was German, or even Nazi, but because it was a phenomenon of western science in general. . . .
>
> In the United States, for example, legalized killing of mentally retarded children was advocated by the American psychiatrist Kennedy in a 1941 presentation to the American Psychiatric Association. His concerns were also published as the lead article in the July 1942 issue of the Association's journal. The concept was endorsed by the editors of the journal. The editorial implied that *parental love for such a child was so morbid as to call for psychiatric treatment.* . . .
>
> Many of Germany's prominent psychiatrists collaborated or participated in the killing, or benefitted from it. . . . Their texts were widely used or cited by American psychiatrists and continue to be even today.
>
> A good number of American psychiatrists were students of the German euthanasia leaders and have in turn become the teachers of *a great many psychiatrists in practice today.*[6]

As Wertham is at pains to make clear,

Another economic gain from mass violence was the use of human beings as test objects for experiments with marketable pharmaceutical products and chemical war weapons such as poison gas. . . .

This industry was designed and organized by scientists and doctors. . . .

These inhuman experiments are not a thing of the past. *They are still taken for granted and commercially cited.*[7]

Most influential was the book *The Release of the Destruction of Life Devoid of Value,* published in Leipzig in 1920 . . . The book advocated that killing of "worthless people" be released from penalty and legally permitted . . . The concept of "life devoid of value" or "life not worth living" was not a Nazi invention, as is often thought. It derives from this book. . . .

The psychiatrist author (Albert Hoche) decries any show of sympathy in such cases, because it would be based on "erroneous thinking." . . .

Hoche was professor of psychiatry and director of the psychiatric clinic at Freiburg from 1902 to 1934. . . . In his clinic a number of eminent specialists were trained—for example, Dr. Robert Wartenberg, who later became one of the outstanding and most popular teachers of neurology in California. . . .[8]

Ernst Reudin was the chief architect of the compulsory sterilization law of 1933. This law was so vigorously formulated and interpreted that, for example, any young man with a harmless phimosis [constriction of the foreskin, a condition easily curable by circumcision or a small surgical incision] was forced to be sterilized. . . . The results of enforced castrations in the period from 1933 to 1945 *are still quoted in current psychiatric literature without any critique* of their inhumanity.[9]

We saw in a previous chapter that the Nazi movement was largely energized by New Age teaching. Nazi leaders were disciples of men who claimed to be guided by unseen spirits. In God's plan, the Nazi movement failed at that time and place. Germany suffered a devastating judgment of fire, famine, and brutal occupation, some of which continues until this day.

Now, the Nazi New Age is back—not with swastikas and anti-Jewish sermons, but with white coats and degrees from prestigious institutions. The message is the same. Even some of the people are the same. Only the facade has changed.

Question Authority

We find it easy today to criticize the German Christians for their weak resistance to Hitler. We find it incredible that large numbers of professing believers would actually have become enthusiastic supporters of a mass murderer. But if we cede the same life-and-death power to experts—doctors, judges, psychiatrists, social scientists—that the Germans gave the Nazis, we are no better than they were.

Just as the answer to Satan's tactic of detoxified language is to start speaking the truth in love, so the answer to New Age idolatry is to recognize and confront the false gods.

Scripturally, "he who would be greatest among you shall be servant of all." This applies to all who want to lead us. God commands doctors, judges, legislators, and other "gods" to *serve*.

Doctors achieved their present status in our culture by acting as servants. We are all familiar with the picture of the old country doctor in his shabby coat, coming on the run in the middle of the night to fight sickness with all his might . . . and sometimes conveniently forgetting the bill later on when the sick one's family could not afford to pay. In those days, doctors were loved and almost revered because of their self-sacrificial behavior.

Now doctors want to be gods—not all doctors, but many of the leaders of the profession. They want *control,* wealth, and power.

Of course, the ultimate goal is that we would *all* become wards of Modern Medicine. Doctors exhibit a dangerous tendency to take advantage of every opportunity to *force* individuals to do things just for the sake of doing them. If doctors didn't want more and more power over the individual, why would more and more medical procedures be showing up as laws? Why should you have to fight with a doctor in order to have your baby at home, breastfeed it, send it to school without immunizations, or treat its illnesses in any manner you believe effective?[10]

The AMA has been successful in that the public now expects doctors to perform miracles and sues at the drop of a hat when the expected miracle fails to arrive. Doctors are not supposed to make *any* mistakes, since they are no longer human beings like the rest of us.

But New Wave doctors are, in fact, somewhat *more* fallible than the rest of us.

Conservative accounts peg the number of psychiatrically disturbed physicians in the U.S. at 17,000 or one in twenty, the number of alcoholics at more than 30,000, and the number of narcotics addicts at 3,500 or one percent. A thirty-year study comparing doctors with professionals of similar socio-economic and intellectual status found that by the end of the study nearly half the doctors were divorced or unhappily married, more than a third used drugs such as amphetamines, barbiturates, or other narcotics, and a third had suffered emotional problems severe enough to require at least ten trips to a psychiatrist. The control group of non-doctors didn't fare nearly as badly.

Doctors are from thirty to one hundred times more likely than lay people to abuse narcotics. . . .

Doctors' suicide rate is twice the average for all white Americans.[11]

Our new gods are not only worse off spiritually than the rest of us; they have quite often been proven wrong before. Look what the standard pediatrics texts advised during the 1920s (an era, by the way, that fostered the first wave of what is now known as the New Age):

The practice of playing with infants and exciting them by sights, sounds, and motions until they shriek with apparent delight is often harmful and should be condemned. Never hug and kiss them. Never let them sit on your lap. If you must, kiss them once on the forehead when they say goodnight. Babies under six months old should never be played with. And of kissing, the less the better. Rocking is forbidden. So are pacifiers. Should the child attempt to pacify himself by sucking his thumb, pasteboard splints must be applied to his elbows to prevent him from bending his arms. At night his arms must be tied to his sides."[12]

Today, our would-be priests do not show themselves any more infallible than in the past. Not surprisingly, the knife-wielders are leading the way in what can quite plainly be seen as unscientific medical practices. A recent *Insight* article explains:

These studies [of deaths due to hospital-caused infections and errors in drug prescription and dosing] do not acknowledge what Dr. Eugene D. Robin of Stanford University says may be the largest category of iatrogenic [doctor-caused] disease. These are systematic errors introduced into medicine, and widely used on patients, which result in harm or death to masses of patients," says Robin. He calls this category iatroepidemics. . . .

Unnecessary surgery is also a major iatroepidemic, says Robin . . .

Inlander and his coauthors [in their book *Medicine on Trial*] estimate the annual death toll in the United States from unnecessary surgery is 40,000 to 83,000.

These problems are by no means restricted to surgery. In a study for the Washington-based National Leadership Commission on Health Care, Dr. David Eddy found that for many medical practices, there is virtually no scientific evidence of effectiveness.[13]

"For many medical practices there is virtually no scientific evidence of effectiveness." The same could be said about the practices of the other "gods" of our society: judges (who are never impeached even when they have clearly sabotaged the Constitution), ethicists (who are taken seriously as "scientific moralists" while preachers who quote the Bible are labeled "ultrafundamentalist extremists who want to impose their morality on others"), psychologists (whose testimony is definitive in court even though it is based on unscientific and anti-biblical presuppositions), and so on.

In all these cases, the authority comes "in his own name."

I am not Ashamed of the Gospel

Christians have encountered situations like this before.

In every new pagan tribe, the missionary finds himself up against an existing pagan educational establishment, a pagan mind-set closed to the new message, and an existing authority structure designed to perpetuate paganism.

But missionaries generally know enough to confront pagans with Bible truth. They are not ashamed to quote the Bible as *the* authority. They do not waste time worrying about how to preserve "pluralism" and how to "respect the rights" (or, in this case, the rites) of pagans to follow their own religious bent. They are not afraid to impose the Bible's morality in the place of pagan sacrifices.

If the missionary's message is not received right away, he does not then cave in and accept the pagan way. If he is called names, threatened, or attacked, this does not cause the mission board to endorse paganism out of fear of further reprisals. If he loses his very life (as in the case of the missionaries speared to death by Auca Indians in the 1950s), more come forward to take his place.

Missionaries do all this because they agree with the Apostle Paul: "I am not ashamed of the gospel, because it is the power of God for the salvation of everyone who believes" (Romans 1:16). Where this word is preached, there *is* a harvest. Those God calls *do* get saved. Their lives *do* change. Their culture also changes under the new influence of heavenly salt and light.

If you are white, do you offer sacrifices to Thor, Odin, and the Anglo-Saxon gods? Why not? Didn't your ancestors do so? If you are black, do you follow the ancient tribal rituals of ceremonial torture and sacrifice? Why not? If you are of oriental descent, do you fear the spirits of your ancestors? Why not? The answer, in all cases, is that once upon a time someone preached the gospel to you or your ancestors and taught you or them how Christians should behave.

In the everlasting battle between God and Satan, between the true church and the Whore of Babylon, Christians are guaranteed victory only as long as we fight. "The gates of hell will not prevail" against us, but this only is true if we know enough to attack them. The end, the rule of Antichrist that immediately precedes Jesus' physical return, comes only when "the love of many waxes cold," not when we are faithful and on fire for God.

We have been seduced into trying to be "respectable" . . . trying to fit in to what is becoming an utterly pagan culture. This is impossible. So, if we are going to have to become unrespectable sooner or later, why not do it now and in a big way? Why not be *blatantly* Christian? Why not actually act like missionaries? Why not face down the false gods and idols of this society and trust in God's power to do the rest?

Babylon Is Falling

Idols always have had feet of clay. They are not gods; they are not in control of history. Though pagan idolatry may have its way in certain times and seasons, the Bible tells us that it is ultimately doomed.

> After this I [the Apostle John] saw another angel coming down from heaven. He had great authority, and the earth was illuminated by his splendor. With a mighty voice he shouted:
> "Fallen! Fallen is Babylon the Great! . . .
> Then I heard another voice from heaven say:
> "Come out of her, my people, so that you will not share in her sins, so that you will not receive any of her plagues . . ."
> (Revelation 18:1, 2, 4)

If we confront the idols of our day, "In this world you will have trouble," but in the next world, blessing. The gospel is, after all, an *eternal* message. Babylon is doomed to fail, while God's

Kingdom will go on forever. We do not need to know the times and seasons, since the battle is the same in all ages. Life versus death. Hate versus mercy. Truth versus lies. Christ's sacrifice versus sacrifices to Satan.

Now choose life, so that you and your children may live and that you may love the Lord your God, listen to his voice, and hold fast to him. For the Lord is your life. (Deuteronomy 30:19, 20)

PART V: HOLY SACRIFICES

SEVENTEEN

Servants of All

Whoever wants to be great among you must be your servant, and whoever wants to be first must be your slave—just as the Son of Man did not come to be served, but to serve, and to give his life a ransom for many.

(Matthew 20:25, 26)

But if a widow has children or grandchildren, these should learn first of all to put their religion into practice by caring for their own family and so repaying their parents and grandparents, for this is pleasing to God.

(1 Timothy 5:4)

If anyone does not provide for his relatives, and especially for his immediate family, he has denied the faith and is worse than an unbeliever.

(1 Timothy 5:8)

Christians have no reason to sit still, wringing our hands and fatalistically awaiting a pagan future. In every society where Christians have recognized the culture's pagan features and opposed them, bringing the message of Jesus Christ fearlessly to the people, human sacrifice has ended. We are convinced that the only things preventing this from happening in our own society are:

(1) We have been fooled into seeing paganism as "secular" and "neutral" thanks to the way it is being reintroduced.

(2) We have bought the lie that, for some reason, *in our own culture* Christians should not be missionaries in the same way we are in other cultures. In *this* culture we think we must not say, "Thus saith the Lord," but instead should present "religiously neutral" arguments—which often turn out to be baptized pagan ethics.

(3) We have forgotten the doctrine of revival. We have become prophets of times and days and seasons, trying to pin down the physical return of our Lord, instead of making sure we are found good stewards when He comes. We have allowed ourselves to believe that Satan's final triumph *must* occur now—and that thus it is useless to fight against evil—forgetting that the New Age is nothing more than the Old Age of Babylonian paganism which the church has so often fought and overcome. We project the future based on trends of the past and present, exactly the same way secular newspaper prophets do, instead of looking to God to do a "new thing" and reveal His power once again.

Taking on the New Wave Confederation of Humanists and New Agers: "Show Me" Christians

What will it mean in practice for Christians to challenge the New Wave in medicine?

For one thing, we might hear dialogs like this:

"You're just trying to impose your morality on society!"

"Well, you're just trying to impose your knife on society . . . and God says, 'Thou shalt not kill.'"

Christians would be "Show Me" Christians once again, like the first-century Berean Christians who "examined the Scriptures daily" to check out the Apostle Paul's teaching (Acts 17:11). Instead of automatically hailing each new medical, scientific, or legislative procedure as an "advance," we would remember to ask these questions:

(1) Is it biblical? (If it fails this test, stop right here.)

(2) Does it truly benefit the person for whom it is done, without harming others?

(3) Is it the simplest, least meddlesome solution?

(4) Is there evidence it works?

Back to the Bible

One simple step we can take right now that will really help is to insist on Biblical qualifications rather than secular, paganized credentials as the basis for leadership in our churches.

At the moment, the fastest track to an important position in the church is to get a secular credential. This, however, only entitles the holder to extra authority insofar as he is able to promote the new pagan agenda behind his credential. After all, a Doctor of Philosophy has no automatic advantage over Fred the Plumber when it comes to *Bible* knowledge—and if he admitted that most of his doctorate was obtained soaking up non-Christian ideas, he would have no advantage over Fred at all. Therefore, the Doctor *has* to promote his non-Christian training as good for Christians, or his credential gains him nothing. He even has to promote his training *over* the Bible, or Fred would still be able to overrule the Doctor's authority.

This process is a wide-open pipeline for deliberate infiltration of the church by pagans—and feminists, witches, and New Agers have all gone on record as stating they intend to infiltrate and take over our churches.[1] They would find this chore a lot harder if we required Biblical qualifications from those who would be teachers in the church: a good character, sanctified home life, sound doctrine, and wide Bible knowledge.

Sticks and Stones May Break My Bones, or Who Cares What the New York Times Says?

Challenging the New Wave also means Christians would worry less about being called names, and get on with our business of living and proclaiming Bible truth. If we have to have endorsements from every secular media outlet before we will dare to take a stand on anything, we might as well give up right now!

Because Christians, by very nature, tend to prefer avoiding quarrels, we often back down when we see the opposition getting annoyed. It might help to remember what John Wesley used to ask his evangelists when they returned from a tour.

"Did anyone get saved?" he would inquire.

If an evangelist reluctantly reported that nobody made a profession of faith, Wesley would ask the next question:

"Well, did anyone get *angry?*"

Wesley knew that anger is one of the first signs that an unregenerate heart is becoming convicted of its unrighteousness. People get angry because they feel threatened—because they sense defeat! When you see New Wave "authorities" begin to rant and rave about "those cursed fundamentalists" who are "interfering with progress," you will know we are on the right track. As Jesus said,

Blessed are you when people insult you, persecute you, and falsely say all kinds of evil against you because of me. Rejoice and be glad, because great is your reward in heaven, for in the same way they persecuted the prophets who were before you. (Matthew 5:11, 12)

"I Was Sick, and You Visited Me"

But defending the helpless chosen victims of pagan sacrifice requires more even than good preaching and a pure church. It requires *ministries of mercy,* so patients have a place to go where they can find compassion and a chance for healing, without any concern about becoming victims of someone's New Wave agenda. In most cases, such patients only need simple nursing care. In other cases, there is a need for high-tech intervention mingled with a solid Christian commitment to fighting for life.

Christians need to face head-on the reality that government (and insurance company) responsibility for medical care produces an "inevitable result: strict federal rationing of health services."[2] If we do not take care of our own families, as the Bible commands us (1 Timothy 5:8), and then reach out "as we have opportunity . . . [to] do good to all people, especially to those who belong to the family of believers" (Galatians 6:10) we can *expect* government to enforce unholy sacrifice. Elite leaders will decide who lives, who dies, and which medical procedures are funded. Your very body will belong to these leaders, as they will be able to invoke "rising costs" and "the benefit of society" to require you to get sterilized, to abort "excess" babies, to donate unborn (or even older) children for experimentation, and to yourself become an involuntary organ donor.

This is what is already happening in countries where the government totally controls medicine, such as Russia and China. It is totally contrary to the Bible's teaching that we are "bought at a price" and should not become "slaves of men" (1 Corinthians 7:23).

Lobbying for increased government funding of medical care for the poor can *not* take the place of providing such care ourselves. Calls for more regulation of nursing homes can *not* substitute for caring for our own parents and elderly relatives. Jesus never commended the righteous by saying, "I was sick, and you urged Caesar to visit me."

Careerism or Ministry?

Careerism—the headlong pursuit of worldly success—is all that stands between the Christian church and our opportunity to take the lead in the medical arena. If singles, mothers and fathers, and older people *all* spend the majority of our time making money, who will be able to care for the sick? We can't very well refuse to take care of our own children and elderly parents and expect unbelievers to show self-sacrificing love for them. We need to recapture the age-old Bible teaching that *ministry* is more blessed than *money,* and that it truly is "more blessed to give than to receive" (Acts 20:35).

Along these lines, it is about time that the church recognized that stay-at-home wives *are* working wives. These women Biblically form the backbone of the Christian mercy ministry corps. Every ill family member that we care for ourselves at home is one less excuse for New Wave leaders to set up a mass murder program. This does not mean that Christian wives can't have other ministries as well. In fact, one of us wrote a book detailing the astonishingly varied ministries God has given to home-centered wives and mothers (Mary Pride, *The Way Home*, Crossway Books, 1985). But it does mean that the church will have to make a conscious decision to return to the Biblical pattern of *personal* ministry, rather than continuing to hand over more and more of our ministries to secular institutions.

A combination of family ministry (caring for our own family members) and group ministry (caring for those who have no family) is needed, and both those who make medical ministry their official calling and those who quietly take it on as part of their housework are worthy of honor.

If we want to lead society back to biblical principles of mercy and caring, we as a church have to once again become "servants of all" (Matthew 20:26).

Now we have some good news for you! Christian history shows us exactly how to go about setting up medical ministries—because Christians *pioneered* nursing care in Western civilization.

EIGHTEEN

Blessed Are the Merciful

I always dressed all the wounds every morning, and I soon found that my grief and sorrow were forgotten in administering to the wants of the sick. Such patience and fortitude I have never seen. Not one murmur did I ever hear escape the lips. My Prayer Book was my constant companion. I carried it in my pocket and many poor soldiers have I soothed and comforted with Holy prayers.

(From the diary of Mrs. Annie K. Kyle of
North Carolina, a "frail woman on crutches"
who became head nurse in the hospital
at Fayetteville during the Civil War)

Blessed are the merciful, for they shall obtain mercy.

(Matthew 5:7)

Jesus Christ came "healing the sick and driving out demons." His first followers immediately took up this work as well. The Apostles Peter, John, and Paul are all credited with healing miracles, and they in turn left instructions for permanent ministries of healing within the church. These included communal and private prayers for healing (James 5:16), the ministry of the elders in anointing the sick with oil and praying for him in faith (James 5:14), the ministry of older women and deaconesses (1 Timothy 5:9, 10), and special gifts of healing (1 Corinthians 12:9, 28, 30). Part of the training of younger women likely also included home nursing skills, as these were necessary virtues for a charitable woman.

The practical effects of this Bible teaching in the early church was the founding of special offices for widows, virgins, deacons, and deaconesses.

The canons or decisions of certain Church councils and synods speak directly of these Church officers also. They indicate that at certain periods the widows and virgins wore a distinctive dress, took the vow of chastity, and sometimes lived in their own homes, from which they went out to do good works; on other occasions they lived in monasteries.[1]

Source documents from these early times testify freely to the consecration of these early nurses, and the love that their patients felt for them.

This happy state persisted into the Middle Ages, when several eminent saints were famous for their acts of medical mercy. This number includes Francis of Assisi and Clare of Assisi, Catherine of Siena, and Elizabeth of Hungary. Elizabeth, the daughter of the King of Hungary, gave up all rights to the throne and devoted herself to building hospitals and personally caring for the most unlovely of the sick.

These four "nursing saints" but exemplify the many men and women who, in this era, lived lives of devotion to the sick and needy of their communities, and whose influence was felt widely in succeeding ages.[2]

Under the Catholic Church, orders of nuns and monks were formed for the express purpose of caring for the sick. Secular nurses were also available for caring for patients in the patients' own homes.

Following the Protestant Reformation, Protestant religious

nursing orders sprang up. These did not require lifelong vows of celibacy, as did the Catholic nursing orders, but were structured very similarly. Groups of single people of one sex came together under the headship of an older, more experienced member of their sex. Together, they devoted themselves full-time to the care of the sick.

A major revival of this system of care in modern times began through the work of Pastor Theodor Fliedner of Kaiserwerth in Germany. This Christian deaconess system spread throughout Protestant countries. The deaconess movement was particularly strong in England, where it became a part of the Established Church under the title of "sisterhoods." The sisters were sometimes called Protestant Sisters of Charity.

Florence Nightingale, a single woman of considerable talents and a fine family background, who is usually considered the moving force behind the modern nursing profession, was profoundly influenced by Kaiserwerth. Miss Nightingale plainly picked up the concept of nursing as a calling and ministry, rather than as a career, quite early in her own life, and her dedication to this principle was largely responsible for the massive public support for her attempts to reform nursing in her day.

In North America, religious nursing communities patterned after the European model made an early appearance. As early as the sixteenth century, French Jesuit and Recollet missionaries had "erected rude buildings in Quebec and Montreal for the purpose of caring for the Indians, [which] later grew into imposing hospitals . . . the patients being nursed by orders of nuns and canonesses."[3] Things moved a bit slower among Protestants, who originally cared for the sick on a neighbor-helping-neighbor basis, and whose hospitals were first set up by government or by companies (such as the Dutch West India company) for the care of their employees. However, starting in the mid-1800s,

Protestant Episcopal sisterhoods also entered the field with the Sisterhood of the Holy Communion, founded in New York in 1845 by Pastor Muhlenberg. . . . Nursing work under the auspices of the English Lutheran Church in the United States began when four deaconesses were brought to Pittsburgh to Pastor Passavant's Hospital in 1849, by Pastor Fliedner of Kaiserwerth.[4]

Pastor Muhlenberg tells how and why his congregation founded a sisterhood and hospital.

On St. Luke's Day, 1846, the want of a church hospital in this city was laid before the congregation . . .

Before this, however, much thought had been given to the plan and practical working of the projected institution. In order that it might have a genuine Christian character, it was felt that its beneficiaries must be chiefly in the care of volunteers . . . and they, Christian women, waiting upon the sick and needy for the Lord's sake. . . . Why could we not have . . . Sisters here, and in our *own* church?

The question was presented to an earnest Christian woman, who alone of all my acquaintances was likely to listen to it with any thought of acting upon it. The result . . . was the devotion of a life to the voluntary ministrations of Christian love, especially among the poor . . . This single volunteer, in the course of a twelvemonth or more, was joined by two others as probationers, and thus there was the germ of a community.[5]

This broad mix of nursing care—self-care, family care, neighbor care, visiting nurse care, and organized Christian care—persisted as time went on. The Civil War led to a greater demand for organized nursing, which was met according to the old system of nurses (mainly single women) devoting themselves full-time to the care of the sick and wounded. The American Medical Association, noting the superior results when single people entered upon nursing as a ministry, issued this report in 1869:

While it is not at all essential to combine religious exercises with nursing, it is believed that such a union would be eminently conducive to the welfare of the sick in all public institutions; and the

Committee therefore earnestly recommend the establishment of
nurses' homes, to be placed under the immediate supervision and
direction of deaconesses, or lady superintendents, an arrangement
which works so well in the nurses' homes at London, Liverpool,
Dublin, and other cities in Europe, and at the Bishop Potter
Memorial House in Philadelphia.[6]

Medical Missions

The modern missions movement also made, and still makes, great
efforts to bring medical care to non-Christian cultures. Commonly,
the missionary himself and his wife became doctors and nurses by
necessity. Armed perhaps with only a few of the most basic drugs
and medicines, a syringe, some sutures, bandages, and a First Aid
textbook, they would find themselves assisting at childbirth,
sewing up gashes, attending the infirm and dying, and tangling
with parasitic infections, tuberculosis, malaria, and a host of other
diseases. Soon they would be begging for real doctors and nurses
to come and set up a clinic—a response which often was heeded.
So today, even in countries where Christian evangelism is supposedly strictly forbidden, such as the lands of Islam, we find Christian medical missions ministering to the sick and sharing the faith
of Jesus Christ.

A Time to Heal

Only lately, as the West has grown rich (enabling people to pay for
work formerly done as a ministry) and technologically arrogant
(causing amoral technique to replace the former credential of
wholehearted commitment to the care of the sick), has nursing
ceased to be a Christian calling. Interventionist doctoring has now
replaced the former primary emphasis on providing an environment in which God can do the healing. Nurses are seen more and
more as human robots whose only function is to carry out the doctor's orders—which today may say, "Do not feed or provide liquids."

The time has clearly come for Christians once again to take
the leading role in care of the sick. We can do this the same way

Christians always have done so through the centuries: through home nursing, neighbor nursing, and official church ministries of mercy.

Home Nursing and Health Literacy

The government (public) schools now teach health and sometimes very simple first aid. Unhappily, these schools are controlled by the same people responsible for the current epidemic of pagan thinking in our culture. The courses may go so far as to endorse deathmaking (via euthanasia and abortion). In any case, the only health skills they ever teach are emergency skills. Even in the simplest matters students are advised to turn over all medical care to a physician or hospital. Often no reason is given for *why* a particular action is medically helpful or harmful—students are just told to take it on authority. There is also no encouragement of long-term personal nursing—for example, nursing of elderly relatives.

Christian schools and home schools, therefore, now have a wide open field in the matter of teaching basic nursing to their students. Since we all have bodies, and all either will be sick ourselves at some time or will have sick or old family members who need care, it makes sense to make Christian nursing—or "health literacy"—a part of the basic curriculum. Some time currently spent on less-crucial matters (e.g., making seashell collages) could be set aside to demonstrate care of the bedfast: how to make a bed while the sick person stays in it, how to prevent or treat bedsores, how to prepare food for the very ill, and so on.

Since no law prevents teaching or learning about even the most advanced medical procedures, there is no reason why health literacy should not include the most advanced personal medical technology, such as how to insert and care for an IV, how to set up and use an oxygen tent, how to monitor blood pressure and administer simple home tests, and so on. It would also be a good idea to present and contrast the major types of medical care, such as chiropractic, homeopathy, naturopathy, nutritional counseling, and so forth, instead of focusing solely on allopathy (conventional medicine). Because allopathy has broken away from its previous scientific moorings and become saturated with pagan concepts, it must be restored by those who have a secure Biblical foundation. All these types of medicine should be critiqued in view of Biblical principles, giving the students a chance to see that medicine, like other areas of life, is under the authority of God. The curriculum also should include a lengthy treatment of the role of prayer, encouragement, and a cheerful heart in healing, and the importance of a sweet, servantlike attitude on the part of the medical caregivers, as well as concentrating on the fact that *God* heals and we can only remove obstacles to healing. Students should know that drugs and scalpels are not the only way to treat medical problems, and that every sick person does not automatically belong in a hospital.

Neighbor Nursing

This used to be called "visiting the sick," and mainly involves such forms of service as bringing over meals, doing laundry, and generally helping out while the patient's own family does the bulk of the nursing. In cases where the patient has no family, and it is impractical or unwise for the patient to be in a hospital, a godly church member who has been trained in home nursing could be encouraged to take the patient in as a ministry.

Ministries of Mercy

These are large-scale works designed to provide an outlet for single people to devote themselves full-time to ministry. The Bible says that the single state is better only if the single person is free to consecrate himself or herself 100 percent to serving the Lord. Today we have largely lost that vision, as Christian magazines and books concentrate on teaching singles how to succeed in the secular workforce. This means each single person has the burden of providing his or her own home, car, appliances, and so on, a burden which often wipes out their ability to be productive anywhere *but* their job. It also forces the single person to demand a much higher salary than would be necessary if housing, transportation, and so on were provided as part of his work.

The religious nursing orders of the past made it possible for the church to send large numbers of workers out into the medical harvest field without exhausting her resources. These workers lived at the nursing location, looked upon their work as a ministry, and consequently were able to do a lot for a very little amount of money. Since the church supported their work, they were able to minister to the poor without any fear of "wasting scarce resources" by not extracting every nickel from their patients. Their work provided them with a community where they could experience the joys of sisterhood or brotherhood without needing a wife or husband. The effectiveness of this structure can be seen in the fact that in such orders where lifelong vows were not required, workers nonetheless often spent their entire lives in this service. Mother Teresa of Calcutta is an example of how this concept still works today.

In His Steps

The situation literally is desperate. Thousands are being sent into eternity from non-Christian hospices where the gospel is actively discouraged and a belief in reincarnation is fostered. Tens of thousands are being starved and dehydrated to death because the medical establishment refuses to encourage compassion, or do the work to make it real. Hundreds of thousands are neglected or abused to death through poor quality or deliberately hostile nursing care. And this is just the tip of the iceberg. If someone doesn't jump in and show that compassion *works,* death will become the medical procedure of choice.

We can preach, and we can pray, but we need to do more. We need to do the works of our Master . . . to follow in His steps. Our work does not have to be fancy or elaborate—indeed, there are good reasons to keep it simple and tie it directly to the home and the existing ministry of the local church. We don't need to begin by sending out a call for Christians to infiltrate and take over medical schools, a process which, even if successful, would take a dozen years to begin to bear fruit. We can start *where we are* by feeding the hungry, clothing the naked, taking in the stranger, visiting the sick. A cup of cold water today is worth ten tons of cold water tomorrow if our patient is going to die of neglect or as the victim of sacrificial surgery in the meantime.

Wanted: Heroes

We could, in fact, use more than consecrated Christian nurses and doctors. Somehow the Christian community needs to rise up and rescue the present victims of unholy sacrifice.

The church had this opportunity once before in recent history and blew it. Let's look quickly at what the German Christians did and why it did not work.

> There were few heroes in this sorry chapter of history. . . . Major opposition did come from the pastors who directed institutions and from the churches. However, even much of this opposition was flawed. It was: (a) slow in coming, (b) restrained in expression, and (c) just as *neat* as the extermination in that it pursued administrative, legal and other normative channels of recourse. For instance, a major memorandum from a major Protestant church leader protested that the killing violated due process— rather than the law of God. A pastor-administrator of one of the affected institutions similarly focussed his protest on the illegality rather than immorality of the killing. *I have not yet discovered a sufficient documentation of persons having taken a prophetic stand such as actually blocking the doorway to the henchmen or offering themselves in lieu of a handicapped person.* (emphasis ours)[7]

The German Christians' opposition to Nazi human sacrifice was

(1) slow in coming

(2) restrained in expression

(3) and limited to "respectable" protests following the same legal and administrative channels that had authorized the Holocaust in the first place.

We would do well not to imitate the Germans. Instead, we have a stirring example of how Christians really should respond to human sacrifice in the pro-life direct action movement. These are the people who, defying the unconstitutional laws preventing access to abortion-headed women, trespass on parking lots and enter abortion clinics to speak directly to the women. They confront the abortionists directly at home and at work, hold prayer vigils outside the clinics, and wherever possible stage massive sit-ins that prevent all abortions in a clinic while the sit-in lasts. Many lives have been saved as a result of this movement, as women have had the chance to hear a message and *see* that these Christians really believe it and are willing to pay the price. Even abortionists have gotten saved and given up their gruesome work! Perhaps the only reason we have not already seen God's judgment descend on our culture has been that people such as pro-life direct activists have provided America with salt that Germany was lacking. Here we *have* our heroes who will block the doorway and offer themselves as sacrifices to the legal system rather than sit by while the killing continues.

It is just the beginning of the New Age of medicine. The system is not yet thoroughly entrenched or compulsory. A few hundred Christians, no more than the membership of most local churches, if we were willing to invade the hospitals where a Nancy Ellen Jobes or a Claire Conroy is about to be murdered, could in God's grace turn the tide of this deadly movement.

Is There a Doctor in the Household of Faith?

Mass protests against medical murder may be needed—but the need for such protests can be greatly reduced if Christians in the medical professions band together and take a stand *as Christians* against these sorts of practices.

This is a time of tremendous opportunity and risks for Christian doctors. The opportunity is there to take a historically significant "stand in the gap" against paganized medicine and for the old ethics of compassion, benefit to the patient, and a servant attitude towards the patient. Not every medical person, whether Christian or nonbeliever, finds it easy to swallow the direction modern medicine is taking. There is a great deal of confusion and soul-searching going on, as the following quotes from a lengthy article on medical ethics testify.

But when doctors use people as guinea pigs, as they have done with both Baby Fae and Bill Schroeder, at what point does the

urge to advance science conflict with their duty to care for the
sick?

High technology costs a bundle, and already decisions are
being made that determine who dies and who has a chance for
life. Ultimately, those choices may lie between spending money
to keep an aging population alive or permitting— perhaps even
encouraging—euthanasia. Is there any way to make such decisions fair? . . .

Says University of Rochester ethicist Colleen Clements, "We
call all this medical ethics, but *there is in fact no good ethical
theory there at all.* Especially with biological issues, what you
get is ethics case by case." . . .

There's *no clear ethical means of choosing* when any decision will end in someone's death; the only guideline that Fineberg
(dean of the Harvard School of Public Health) can suggest is "the
particular physician cannot decide not to treat—he has an ethical
obligation to the patient before him. Therefore, society has to
provide an overarching decision. *Currently, society lacks the will
or the mechanism to do so.*" . . .

In fact, *almost none of the ethical questions raised by the
advances of high technology and transplant medicine have clear
answers.* (emphasis ours)[8]

This period of indecision, when voices still are allowed to
challenge the New Wave, won't last forever. Society will make up
its mind one way or another. Now is the window of opportunity,
when brave Christians already in the medical professions have a
real chance to make a difference.

Opportunities in Alternative Medicine

If you are practitioner in an alternative medical field, such as
homeopathy or chiropractic or midwifery, you are already in a
good position. These disciplines at present all stress the importance of avoiding unnecessary medical intervention, and follow the
old Christian position of admiring God's design in enabling the
body to heal itself rather than a "miracle-working" attitude. Your
job will be more to resist any new professionalizing trends in your

field leading to arrogance on the part of its practitioners than to combat any actual deathmaking activities. You also are in a position to provide instant alternatives to the neglect-and-knife practices increasingly common in mainstream medicine. To say this is not to automatically endorse every tenet of alternative medicine; just to realize that it has already to some extent become an escape hatch from the inhumanity of New Wave medicine.

The danger in these alternative fields is the influx of New Age believers into these professions. Many "new" techniques of alternative medicine, like visualization therapy and meditation, are simply Old Age paganism and demon-worship warmed over slightly and dressed in scientific-appearing garments. Since these are precisely the portions of alternative medicine that mainstream medicine seems eager to adopt, Christian practitioners of alternative medicine can also make a real contribution by exposing the religious nature of these New Age techniques and taking public positions against their use.

Opportunities in Mainstream Medicine

What if you are not a practitioner of alternative medicine, but a genuine card-carrying member of the AMA? What can you do, realistically, in your present position?

Mainstream doctors know that heavy penalties await those who step out of line with the rest of the profession. Chiropractors, for instance, just recently won a lawsuit against the AMA alleging that the AMA ordered its members to downgrade and socially snub chiropractors, with a view to wiping out the entire chiropractic movement. This sort of coercive manipulation of doctors by medical leaders is apparently quite common. In Missouri, we have personally heard that doctors are now afraid to provide backup service for nurse-midwives because they have been warned that any doctor providing this service will have his hospital privileges yanked. A lawsuit on this issue is now pending. None of this coercive activity on the part of medical leaders is legal. However, since mainstream medicine is a self-policing profession, those in charge of the medical bureaucracy have the power, should they so wish, to act like a medical mafia.

Doctoring is not like other fields, in that most doctors start their careers heavily indebted and totally dependent on the availability of hospital privileges for survival. In addition, if a doctor loses his license, it becomes illegal for him to practice his own trade, even if his patients still want his services. On top of this, the excruciatingly high price of malpractice insurance makes doctors afraid to do anything that is not in the orthodox AMA pattern. If a doctor can show in court that he treated the plaintiff according to accepted medical practice, he will win the lawsuit. If, however, he has departed from the jots and tittles of the AMA's currently endorsed way of doing things, he is liable. These forces—indebtedness, the need for hospital privileges, the fear of losing one's license to practice, and the dangers involved in bucking the current medical trend—have so far kept most doctors in line, even when the AMA abuses its authority.

The AMA has become a law unto itself under these circumstances. Writing in the *Oregonian* of April 13, 1987, Dr. Charles W. Norris explained that the famous AMA position that food and water are now medical care that can ethically be denied patients was not a decision of the physicians of the AMA, but simply that of a small elite in the leadership.

The physicians and ethicists on the Judicial Council handed down this ruling without debate or vote of the AMA membership. The ruling is binding upon the AMA membership despite the fact that the ruling was arrived at by fiat and the actions sanctioned by it are illegal, at least in Oregon.[9]

Solidly Christian doctors are a small minority of the professing Christians with medical degrees, who themselves are a small minority in the profession. So far, attempts to band Christian doctors together have been less than successful, with the Christian Medical Society, for example, unable to issue an unambiguously pro-life statement on such a simple issue as abortion. The solution may be for Christian doctors and other medical workers to forge links to Christians *outside* the medical profession. This gives Christian doctors a way to take their cause to the church, and from there to the society as a whole. It also makes it harder for Christian doctors to be persecuted "in a corner." This tactic works in all kinds of situations where one group of Christians is held hostage in a hostile environment. A major example is the effect of letter-writing campaigns on the freedom of Christian prisoners of conscience in Russia. When the authorities learn that those outside their system are observing their actions, they have incentive to become more lenient to dissenters within the system.

Several steps have already been taken in this direction. One such step was the founding of the *Journal of Biblical Ethics in Medicine* (address given in the Resources section). Another was the statement recently issued by a combined group of physicians, theologians, and lawyers condemning the AMA's position on withholding food and water from those labeled as "terminal." This latter development is so encouraging that we give you part of the story in full.

More than 100 noted theologians, physicians, and lawyers have signed a statement decrying the trend toward withholding artificial feeding from seriously ill patients. . . .

"Deliberately to deny food and water to an innocent human being in order to bring about his death is homicide, for it is the adoption by choice of a proposal to kill by starvation and dehydration," said the 5000-word statement. "Such killing can never be morally right and ought never be legalized."

The statement appears in the March 24 edition of *Issues in Law and Medicine*, a journal of the National Legal Center for the Medically Dependent and Disabled, which is headquartered in Terre Haute, Indiana. Published along with it were similar policy statements adopted by several handicapped-rights groups, including the American Association for Retarded Citizens.

Among those joining in the appeal were Rev. Richard Halverson, chaplain of the U.S. Senate; Robert Destro, attorney and member of the U.S. Commission on Civil Rights; Rev. Richard John Neuhaus, a leading commentator on religion and society; recently deceased Protestant bio-ethicist Paul Ramsey; and Harvard Medical School professor Micheline Mathew-Roth. . . .

The statement also rejected the argument that feeding tubes

are "excessively burdensome" to patients in comas or persistent vegetative states. In separate statements, Neuhaus and [William] May [a professor of moral theology at Catholic University of America and coordinator of the panel that drafted the statement] charge that this is not the "real reason behind the trend. It's not that tube feeding is so burdensome; it's that the continued life of the unconscious person is deemed burdensome by some."[10]

The Christian doctors we have contacted freely admit that they are working their way out of the presuppositions taught in medical school and making mistakes along the way. Just as the Israelites leaving Egypt brought some Egyptian baggage along with them, it may be a while before Christian doctors are really ready to make a full contribution theologically. One such doctor, who has written a book on medical ethics, admitted to one of us that he has repudiated some of the stands he took in that book after deeper Biblical study. What is needed is for Christian medical workers of all stripes—alternative and mainstream practitioners, doctors and nurses—to bring the problems in their profession under the oversight of the church.

We are all in this together. We each will need medical care at some point, and we each will have the opportunity to offer medical care at some point. The homeworker nursing her baby through the flu or taking care of Grandma; the church ladies visiting a new mom and bringing along a hot dinner; the child sponging Grandpa's forehead and bringing him a cooling drink; the husband gently helping his wife into her wheelchair and hand-feeding her dinner; the doctor refusing on principle to withhold food and water from a sick old man; the single woman who chooses to devote her life to the care of the sick as a ministry; the pastor who leads a protest against the starvation of a Nancy Jobes; the missionary who finds himself the chief medical resource in his area—all these, and more, are ministers of mercy. And the darker and more heartless the world outside becomes, the brighter will shine the light of the saints of God.

"Is this not the kind of fasting I have chosen:
to loose the chains of injustice
    and untie the cords of the yoke,
to set the oppressed free
    and break every yoke?
Is it not to share your food with the hungry
    and to provide the poor wanderer with shelter—
when you see the naked, to clothe him,
    and not to turn away from your own flesh and blood?
Then your light will break forth like the dawn,
    and your healing will quickly appear . . ."

> The mouth of the Lord has spoken.
> (Isaiah 58:6-8, 14)

RESOURCES

Magazines, Conferences, and Speakers

A.L.L. *About Issues*
Subscription Department
P.O. Box 1350
Stafford, VA 22554
Make check out to "American Life League."
Subscription: $24.95 per year. Free sample issue available on request.

Best all-purpose pro-life magazine around. Covers all angles, including the New Wave topics of euthanasia, transplants, etc., with special emphasis on abortion. Supports direct action as well as other nonviolent political strategies. Catholic emphasis. Color tabloid, professionally typeset. Books and tapes available. Speaker's bureau.

InterNational Association of Parents and Professionals for Safe Alternatives in Childbirth (NAPSAC)
Route 1, Box 646
Marble Hill, NO 63764
Establishes and assists home birth support groups all over the world.
NAPSAC NEWS included in membership of $15 USA, $17 other countries, or professional membership of $35 USA, $37 other countries.

Pro-life, pro-family organization opposing the New Wave as it applies to pregnancy and birth. Wonderful mail-order bookstore with a wide range of books on childbirth. No religious affiliation. Free book catalog for large SASE. Occasional conferences. Videos of last conference available for $39.95 plus $1 shipping—VHS only.

Journal of Biblical Ethics in Medicine
1050 Clarendon Avenue
Florence, SC 29501
Quarterly. Subscription: $16.

First and only (to our knowledge) attempt to bring medicine back under the tutelage of Scripture. Editors and Board are all medical doctors. A publication of the Forum for Biblical Ethics in Medicine, Inc., which also sponsors conferences on the subject. Christian. Tapes and books available. Not overly technical, but assumes some basic medical knowledge. Quality typesetting and paper.

The People's Doctor Newsletter
P. O. Box 982
Evanston, IL 60204
Monthly. Subscription: $24.

Newsletter founded by the late Dr. Robert Mendelsohn. Pro-family medical advice, highly insightful reporting on New Wave medical trends, advocate for Judeo-Christian medical ethics. Easy reading, friendly. Not at all "fringe" or strange—just lots of common sense. Quality typesetting and paper. Back issues available for $2.50 each. Ask for Volume 12, No. 4 for a shocking look at how the Hastings Center plans to eradicate your religious freedom (and your right to live) under the guise of "scientifically" determining when death occurs. This issue also occurs info on the AMA and "mercy killings," the American Academy of Pediatrics' campaign to eliminate your right to treat your children medically according to your religious convictions, fetal transplants, and more.

TIPS
Training Institute
805 South Crouse Avenue
Syracuse, NY 13244-2280
Make checks out to "SU Training Institute"
Subscription: Individual $25 US, $27 Canada, $30 overseas.
Student $15 US, $17 Canada, $19 overseas. Agency $30 US, $32 Canada, $35 overseas.

This is professor Wolf Wolfensberger's newsletter, and the best source around for up-to-date news and analysis of New Wave deathmaking techniques. Stencil quality, but content more than makes up for lack of glitz. Monographs and other helps available. Conferences can be arranged.

Monograph

The New Genocide of Handicapped and Afflicted People. 120 pages. $8 plus $1.50 shipping. Bulk prices available. Make check payable to "Syracuse University Training Institute." Mail to Training Institute at the *TIPS* address above. The transcript of a one-day workshop given by Wolf Wolfensberger's Training Institute at Syracuse University on the subject of "societal deathmaking of devalued people, and especially the handicapped, impaired, and elderly." Topics include:

- How societal devaluation leads to deathmaking
- The many indirect and subtle ways in which people can be made dead, with examples
- How the attachment of death imagery to people invites and legitimates killing them
- How deathmaking is the logical result of the adaptation of a hedonistic value system in our society
- How and why deathmaking is "detoxified," that is, made to appear good, including many examples of such detoxification
- How different forms of deathmaking are connected
- The most common ways in which devalued people in our society are killed, including those under the protection of human services
- Which groups of devalued persons are most at risk of being made dead
- Estimates of the numbers of devalued classes that are made dead
- The toll that deathmaking is taking on society in general
- One set of coherent responses to the ominous reality of widespread contemporary deathmaking
- Guidelines for protecting the lives of people—especially if they are devalued—while they are patients in hospital

Books on Practical Home Health Care

Page Parker and Lois Dietz, R.N. *Nursing at Home: A Practical Guide to the Care of the Sick and the Invalid in the Home* (Crown Publishers: New York). $16.94 postpaid. Written for the layman. Not specifically Christian in outlook, but helpful. Look for it at your public library.

Robert Mendelsohn, M.D. *Confessions of a Medical Heretic.* $5.50.

——————, et. al. *Dissent in Medicine.* $9.95.

——————. *How to Raise a Healthy Child . . . In Spite of Your Doctor.* $9.95.

——————. *MalePractice: How Doctors Manipulate Women.* $10.95.

All Dr. Mendelsohn's books are available from The People's Doctor, 1578 Sherman Ave., Suite 318, Evanston, IL 60201. All prices postpaid.

Mail-Order Source for Books on Life and Death

Sun-Life
Life Issues Bookshelf
Thaxton, VA 24174

Widest selection available of good books and pamphlets on abortion, euthanasia, Living Will, starvation, suicide, infanticide, anti-life organizations, and positive things we can do to challenge all the above. Catalog, $1. These people carry the invaluable *On Understanding "Brain Death"* by Paul Byrne and Paul Quay, quoted frequently in this book ($1.50) plus a more extensive treatment by the same authors entitled *Brain Death: The Patient, the Physician, and Society* ($3). Add 10% shipping. This is the catalog to get if you need to get educated fast on these issues.

Pro-Life Direct Action Organizations

Are you a hero? Or would you just like to help out a hero? Either way, the following groups, all of which engage in *non-violent* civil disobedience, could use your help—donations, prayers, office assistance, or whatever you can do. Some groups hold large rallies at which they actually surround and close down the clinics. All need sidewalk counselors, picketers, and envelope stuffers, as well as volunteers willing to "trespass" in order to get close enough to the abortion-bound women to plead for the lives of their children. *Abortionists fear pro-life direct activists more than any other pro-life ministry,* because these people actually save babies' lives here and now, and force the abortion clinic staff to confront the truth of what they are doing.

Advocates for Life
P. O. Box 13656
Portland, OR 97213
(503) 257-7023

Defenders of Life
P. O. Box 320
Drexel Hill, PA 19026

Feminists for Life
811 E. 47th St.
Kansas City, MO 64110
(816) 753-2130

Life and Family Center
601 1/2 Mall Germain, Suite 201
St. Cloud, MN 56301
(612) 252-2526

Life Support Services
P. O. Box 16849
San Antonio, TX 78216
(512) 662-7334

Project Life
P. O. Box 1180
Binghamton, NY 13902
(607) 723-4012

Pro-Life Action League
6160 N. Cicero
Chicago, IL 60646
(312) 777-2900

Pro-Life Coalition of Southeast Pennsylvania
247 Keswick Ave.
Glenside, PA 19038

Pro-Life Direct Action League
P. O. Box 35044
St. Louis, MO 63135
(314) 863-1022
PDAL is in charge of the direct action network. Contact
PDAL if you can't locate a direct action group in your area.

Pro-Life Non-Violent Action Project
P. O. Box 2193
Gaithersburg, MD 20879
(301) 774-4043

NOTES

CHAPTER 1: *Pagan Sacrifice in the Old Age*

1. (New York: William Morrow, 1981), p. 25, 66.
2. Taken from the recorded confession of a Thug. A. J. Wightman, *No Friends for Travelers* (London: Robert Hale, 1959), cited in Nigel Davies, *Human Sacrifice in History and Today* (New York: William Morrow, 1981), pp. 87-89.
3. Davies, *Human Sacrifice*, pp. 251, 252.
4. Testimony of Mary Jemison, an adopted Iroquois. Cited in Davies, *Human Sacrifice*, p. 253.
5. Davies, *Human Sacrifice*, p. 193.
6. *Ibid.*, p. 21.
7. *Ibid.*, p. 22, 77, etc.
8. *Ibid.*, p. 77.
9. *Ibid.*, p. 73.
10. *Ibid.*, p. 97.
11. Barbara Heins, "Born an Outcast," *In Other Words,* April/May 1988, p. 4.
12. Garry Hogg, *Cannibalism and Human Sacrifice* (New York: Citadel Press, 1966), p. 16.
13. Davies, *Human Sacrifice*, p. 97.

CHAPTER 2: *Power in the Blood*

1. Davies, *Human Sacrifice*, pp. 81, 82.
2. Hugh Steven, *The Man with the Noisy Heart* (Chicago: Moody Press, 1979), p. 34.
3. Davies, *Human Sacrifice*, p. 20.

CHAPTER 3: It's Not Nice to Worship Mother Nature

1. Page 13.
2. *Man, Myth, and Magic* (New York: Marshall Cavendish), Vol. 6, p. 1554, 1556.
3. *The Oregonian,* October 10, 1987.
4. From a speech by Edith Schaeffer at Briarwood Presbyterian Church, Birmingham, Alabama, Spring 1980.
5. (Westchester, IL.: Crossway Books, 1987), p. 27.
6. William Irwin Thompson, *GAIA: A Way of Knowing.* Quoted in *Organic Gardening,* May 1988, p. 18, under the heading "Nature's Way."
7. Maharishi Mahesh Yogi, *Inauguration of the Dawn of the Age of Enlightenment* (Fairfield, Iowa: Maharishi International University Press, 1975), p.47.
8. Karl Binding, professor doctor of law and philosophy, coauthor of *Permitting the Destruction of Unworthy Life,* Part I, Germany, 1920, as quoted by Nat Hentoff, "Rx: No Food, No Water," *Village Voice,* October 6, 1987.
9. Willis W. Harmon, "Rationale for Good Choosing," *Journal of Humanistic Psychology,* Winter 1981.
10. Ruth Montgomery, *Threshold of Tomorrow* (New York: Ballantine/Fawcett Crest, 1982), p. 206.
11. Elasah Drogin, *Margaret Sanger: Father of Modern Society* (New Hope, KY: CUL Publications, 1979).
12. Allan Chase, *The Legacy of Malthus* (New York: Alfred E. Knopf, 1977), pp. 313-316.
13. Karl Binding and Albert Hoche, *Release of the Destruction of Life Devoid of Value.* Translation by R. Sassone, LIFE, 900 N. Broadway, Suite 725, Santa Ana, California 92701, pp. 37-40.
14. Frederic Wertham, *The German Euthanasia Program* (Cincinnati: Hayes Publishing, 1969).
15. *The Oregonian,* March 30, 1987, p. B-2.
16. B. J. Williams, "Head Trip," *Parade Magazine,* August 9, 1987.
17. *Prophesies and Predictions: Everyone's Guide to the Coming Changes,* (Santa Cruz, CA: Unity Press, 1980), pp. 276, 277.
18. David Spangler, *Revelation: The Birth of a New Age,* (Middleton, WI: Lorian Press, 1975), pp.163, 164.
19. Davies, *Human Sacrifice,* pp. 289, 290.

20. *Ibid.*, p. 26.
21. See, for example, David L. Miller, *The New Polytheism: Rebirth of the gods and goddesses,* (New York: Harper & Row, 1974).

CHAPTER 4: *Come, Sweet Death*

1. *American Heritage Dictionary of the American Language* (Boston: Houghton-Mifflin Company, 1981.
2. Elisabeth Kubler-Ross, *Death: The Final Stage of Growth,* (New York: Touchstone, 1975), p. x.
3. *Ibid.*, p. 119.
4. Elisabeth Kubler-Ross, *Questions and Answers on Death and Dying* (New York: Macmillan, 1974), p. 161.
5. *Ibid.*, p. 162.
6. Davies, *Human Sacrifice*, p. 97.
7. A. Gordon, "Reaction to Gibson," August 1984.
8. Richard Baily, *The Dying Patient,* 1970, pp. 281, 291.
9. Wolf Wolfensberger, "Reflections on Gibson's Article, *Mental Retardation,* August 1984.
10. Kubler-Ross, *Death: The Final Stage of Growth,* p. 165.

CHAPTER 5: *Cracking the Weaker Vessels*

1. "Holocaust II?," *Journal of Learning Disabilities,* August-September 1984, pp. 439, 440.
2. *Ibid.*
3. Jill Lawrence, "'Dumping' of Patients Assailed," *Oregonian,* July 23, 1987.
4. "One Miracle, Many Doubts," *Time,* December 10, 1984.
5. Maharishi Mahesh Yogi, *op. cit.*
6. Chicago, Illinois, February 11, 1985.

CHAPTER 6: *Where There's a Will*

1. Paul A. Byrne and Paul M. Quay, *On Understanding "Brain Death"* (Omaha, NE: Nebraska Coalition for Life Educational

Trust Fund, no date given), p. 36.
2. Concern for Dying Brief for Amicus Curiae, in the Matter of Nancy Ellen Jobes.
3. Jane Marnchianes, "Save the Expense?," *Oregonian*, April 13, 1986, p. B-1.
4. Letter from A. J. Levinson, executive director of Concern for Dying, to A. L. Mopntchyk, October 3 1978.

CHAPTER 7: Guardian Angels of Death

1. Salem (OR) Statesman-Journal, March 25, 1987.
2. *Oregonian*, April 13, 1987.
3. Nat Hentoff, "Rx: No Food, No Water," *The Village Voice*, October 6, 1987.
4. Fred Bayles and Scott McCartney, "Guardians of the Elderly,"*Oregonian*, September 20, 1987.
5. *Ibid.*
6. *Ibid.*
7. Bayles and McCartney, "Guardians of the Elderly, Part 2," *Oregonian*, September 21, 1987.
8. Thomas Levinson,"The Heart of the Matter," *Discover*, February 1985.
9. Marrs, *Dark Secrets*, pp. 134, 161.
10. *Ibid.*, p. 161.
11. *Ibid.*, p. 253.
12. Joseph J. Carr, *The Twisted Cross* (LaFayette, LA: Huntington House, 1985), p. 87. Cited in Marrs, *Dark Secrets*, p. 253.

CHAPTER 8: Dance to the Devil

1. *The Leaning Tower of Babel* (Boston: Little, Brown and Company, 1984).
2. Blumenfeld, *op. cit.*
3. *Education Week*, March 5, 1986. Cited in Blumenfeld, *op. cit.*
4. "Death Pill Supported," *Oregonian*, September 1987.
5. Bruce Hilton, "Death: Now It's Getting as Real as Taxes," San Francisco *Examiner*, October 2, 1987.

6. Joyce Price, "Pro-Suicide Activists Call for Right to Assist," Washington *Times,* March 13, 1987.
7. *National Right to Life News,* April 14, 1987. Cited in *TIPS,* June/September 1987, p. 17.

CHAPTER 9: *Euphemasia*

1. *TIPS,* October-December 1987, p. 27.
2. Davies, *Human Sacrifice,* p. 214.
3. *TIPS,* October-December 1987, p. 27.
4. Rita Marker, "A Cruel Death Sentence," *World,* August 31, 1987, p. 4.
5. Richard A. McCormick, "Caring or Starving? The Case of Claire Conroy," *America,* April 6, 1987.
6. From the translation by Dr. Arthur Anderson and Dr. Charles Dibble.
7. Davies, *Human Sacrifice,* pp. 208, 209.
8. Nat Hentoff, "Come Sweet Death," *Village Voice,* September 29, 1987.
9. *About Issues,* May-June, 1987. Cited in *TIPS,* June-August 1987, p. 19.
10. *TIPS,* October-December 1987, p. 27.
11. Suzanne Fields, "Mercy Killings: Up a Slippery Slope," *Insight,* October 7, 1985, p. 79.
12. Wolfensberger, *The Extermination of Handicapped People in World War II Germany, Ethical Issues Revisited.*
13. *TIPS,* June-August 1987, p. 19.
14. *Interim,* April 1987. Cited in *TIPS,* June-August 1987, p. 19.
15. *TIPS,* April 1987.
16. *TIPS,* April 1988, p. 11.
17. *The Age,* May 2, 1987. Cited in *TIPS,* June/August 1987, p. 19.
18. Vladimir Voinovich, *The Anti-Soviet Soviet Union.* Quoted in the brochure promoting this book from Conservative Book Club.
19. *TIPS,* October-December 1987, p. 26.
20. *Op. cit.*

CHAPTER 10: One Small Step for the New Man

1. (New York: Taplanger Publishing Co., 1972), p. 40.
2 Ibid., p. 29.
3. Ibid., p. 43.
4. Ibid., p. 51.
5. Ibid., p. 52.
6. Ibid., p. 54.
7. Ibid., pp. 59, 60.
8. Ibid., pp. 62-64.
9. Ibid., p. 83.
10. Ibid., p. 88.
11. Ibid., pp. 104, 128.
12. Ibid., p. 143.
13. Ibid.
14. Ibid., p. 187.
15. From De Mota Animalum by Borelli, cited in Venzmer, 5000 Years of Medicine, p. 187.
16. Venzmer, 5000 Years, p. 313.
17. Ibid., pp. 346, 347.

CHAPTER 11: The Life of the Flesh

1. Byrne and Quay, On Understanding "Brain Death," p. 31.
2. Kathleen Stein, "Last Rights," Omni, September 1987.
3. Byrne and Quary, On Understanding "Brain Death," pp. 13-15, 27, 28.
4. Ibid., pp. 9, 44.
5. Tom Philip and Joanne Grant, "Brain-Dead Woman Gives Birth."
6. Byrne and Quay, On Understanding "Brain Death," pp. 27, 35.
7. Stein, "Last Rights."
8. Oregonian, December 5, 1985, p. A-1.
9. Stein, "Last Rights."
10. Richard M. Bucke, Cosmic Consciousness (New York: E. P. Dutton, 1901), cited in Marrs, Dark Secrets, p. 125.
11. David Holzman, "Growing Sensitive to Infant Pain," Insight, February 8, 1988, pp. 52-53.
12. Half the letters column of the March 7, 1988 issue of Insight was

taken up with letters arguing the pros and cons of infant pain relief. One man, Andrew J. Rozsa, Ph.D., the clinical coordinator of the Lakeshore Pain Management Center in Birmingham, Alabama ended his letter, "From this perspective [pain as a psycho-sociobiological phenomenon] the question, whether an infant or a young baby suffers or not, remains unanswered." Finally doctor Kanwaljeet S. Anand, the man whose research demonstrating infants' need for anesthesia sparked the original article, had to take up his pen himself in the April 4, 1988 Letters column in order to point out that the dubious psychological approach of worrying about how infants "perceive" pain clouds the clinically-observed fact that babies and infants who receive no anesthesia during surgery demonstrate intense stress reactions and more post-operative complications than babies who do receive anesthesia. Worth noting also is that withholding of anesthesia, in spite of the much safer anesthetics now available, is common in operations on children as old as *fifteen months,* as pointed out in the article, "Growing Sensitive to Infant Pain."

13. See almost any recent issue of *About Issues* for documentation. This information about how aborted babies are exploited, which used to be stoutly denied by the mainstream press, is now finding its way into major news sources, usually as gee-whiz "Isn't this strange" stories (in the case of babies used for art objects) and "Isn't it wonderful what science can do?" stories (in the case of babies exploited for tissue or organs).

14. *U.S. News & World Report,* November 3, 1986, pp. 68-70.

15. *Ibid.*

16. Byrne and Quay, *op. cit.*

CHAPTER 12: The Body Snatchers

1. Davies, *Human Sacrifice,* p. 14.
2. (New York: Citadel Press, 1958), p. 20.
3. Edward Westmarck, *The Origin and Development of the Moral Ideas* (London: Macmillan, 1906), p. 466. Cited in Davies, *Human Sacrifice,* p. 24.
4. Stein, "Last Rights."
5. *Ibid.*

6. Frank Farmer, Springfield (MO) *News Leader,* January 25, 1987.
7. "Marley's Moonlighter" column of February 16, 1987. Cited in *Moneychanger,* May-June 1987, p. 6.
8. Franklin Sanders, *ibid.*
9. *Ibid.*
10. *TIPS,* October-December 1987, p. 21. Original source described as *SHJ,* 15/5/87.
11. Jane Marnchianes, "Save the Expense?," *Oregonian,* April 13, 1986, p. B-1.
12. Stein, "Last Rights."
13. Westmarck, *Origin and Development,* p. 466. Cited in Davies, *Human Sacrifice,* p. 25.
14. *TIPS,* October-December 1987, p. 30.
15. Walter Block, "A Free Market in Kidneys?," *The Freeman,* 1987, p. 308.
16. "Last Rights," p. 117.
17. Patrick O'Neill, "Federal Legislation Could Stimulate Donations of Human Organs," *Oregonian,* October 5, 1987.
18. *Pro-Life News,* May 1987. Cited in *About Issues,* January 1988, p. 11.
19. "It's Sunday in Brazil: Count Your Kidneys," *Manchester Guardian Weekly,* March 10, 1987. Cited in *About Issues,* July-August 1987, p. 14.
20. Stein, "Last Rights."
21. Hogg, *Cannibalism and Human Sacrifice,* p. 18.
22. From a speech given on November 14, 1987, at a seminar of ex-abortion providers sponsored by the Chicago-based Pro-Life Action League. Reported in the newsletter of Life Support Services, PO Box 791987, San Antonio TX 78279. Jan 22, 1988.
23. *Ibid.*
24. *TIPS,* June-August 1987, p. 6.

CHAPTER 13: *And They Sacrificed Their Children to Molech*

1. Quoted by Ellen Goodman, "'Harvesting' for Organs Goes Too Far," *Oregonian,* December 11, 1987.
2. "Mom Hopes Baby Helps Others Live," Associated Press story, *Statesman/Journal* (Oregon), December 12, 1987.

3. Pages 94-101.
4. Hogg, *Cannibalism and Human Sacrifice,* p. 100.
5. "Case of Infant Organ Donor Poses Dilemma," *Oregonian,* October 29, 1987, p. E-2.
6. Goodman, "Harvesting."
7. "First Word," *Omni,* page 8.
8. "Case of Infant Organ Donor Poses Dilemma."
9. Wolfensberger, "The Extermination of Handicapped People in World War II Germany," *Mental Retardation,* 1981, Volume 19, No. 1, pp. 1-7.
10. Wolfensberger, guest editorial, "A Call to Wake Up to the Beginning of a New Wave of 'Euthanasia' of Severely Impaired People," *Education and Training of the Mentally Retarded,* October 1980, pp. 171-173.
11. Wolfensberger, "Extermination."
12. Frederic Wertham, M.D. *The German Euthanasia Program* (Cincinnati: Hayes Publishing, n.d.), excerpted from *A Sign for Cain: An Explanation of Human Violence* (New York: Macmillan, 1966), p. 52.
13. Arthur H. Matthews, "Ethicists Concerned After Quintuplets' Birth, Tissue Use in Mexico," *World,* January 25, 1988, pp. 4, 5.
14. "Tissue Transplants from Aborted Fetuses: A Moral Dilemma," *Columbus* (OH) *Dispatch,* August 30, 1987, p. 8-H. Note the typical "moral dilemma" pose in the headline of this article. This just means, "We don't think it's wrong to do this, but some people will object, and we don't want to get any flack for standing by our convictions."
15. *TIPS,* October-December 1987, p. 15.
16. "Case of Infant Organ Donor Poses Dilemma" *op. cit.*
17. "Couple Want to Keep Baby Alive as Donor," Associated Press story, *Orlando Sentinel,* December 6, 1987, p. A-10.
18. "Handicapped Baby Dies, Organs are 'Harvested,'" *World,* March 7, 1988, p. 11.
19. Wolfgang Holzgreve, *et. al.,* "Kidney Transplantation from Anencephalic Donors," *New England Journal of Medicine,* April 23, 1987, pp. 1069, 1070.
20. "Mom Hopes Baby Helps Others Live," *op. cit.*
21. Bernard Nathanson, from his talk, "Political Prisoners of Abortion," at the 1987 American United for Life Forum. *The*

Advocate, February 1988, p. 4. Originally printed in *Pro-Life Action News.*

22. Robert Lee Hotz, "New Strides, Hard Choices in Genetics," *Atlanta Journal and Constitution,* April 26, 1987.
23. *Journal of Biblical Ethics in Medicine.* Cited in *World,* January 25, 1988, p. 5.

CHAPTER 14: *Terms of Surrender*

1. Margaret Sanger, *The Pivot of Civilization* (New York: Brentano's, 1922), p. 122.
2. *Ibid.,* p. 100.
3. *Ibid.,* p. 25.
4. *Ibid.,* p. 29.
5. *Ibid.,* pp. 96, 97.
6. *Ibid.,* p. 219.
7. *Ibid.,* p. 271.
8. *Ibid.,* p. 219.
9. *Ibid.,* p. 172.
10. Hoche and Binding, *Release of the Destruction of Life,* p. 17.
11. *Ibid.,* p. 36.
12. "Should Critically Handicapped Newborn Babies be Treated?," *USA Today,* April 1985.
13. *Psychological Seduction* (Nashville: Thomas Nelson Publishers, 1983), p. 126.
14. R. Weir, "Selective Nontreatment of Handicapped Newborns: Moral Dilemmas in Neonatal Medicine," (Don Mills, Ontario: Oxford University Press, 1984).
15. Foster Kennedy, "The Problem of Social Control of the Congenital Defective: Education, Sterilization and Euthanasia," *American Journal of Psychiatry,* July 1942, p. 13. This man was honored by the Nazi-controlled Heidelberg University in 1936, eight years before this article appeared.
16. Hayden Shurtleff, "Lower Myelodysplasia: Decision for Death or Disability," *New England Journal of Medicine,* 1975, pp. 1005-1011.
17. Wolfensberger, "Extermination of Handicapped People," *op. cit.*

CHAPTER 15: Idols in White Coats

1. Marnchaines, "Save the Expense?," *op. cit.*
2. Davies, *Human Sacrifice*, p. 15.
3. *Ibid.*
4. Dr. Robert Mendelsohn, *Confessions of a Medical Heretic* (New York: Warner Books, 1979), p. 17.
5. *Ibid.,* p. 201.
6. *Ibid.,* p. 186.
7. *Ibid.,* p. 185.
8. *Ibid.,* pp. 187, 188.
9. *Ibid.,* pp. 193-195.
10. Davies, *Human Sacrifice*, p. 27.
11. Mendelsohn, *Confessions*, p. 105.

CHAPTER 16: Knives of Steel, Hearts of Marble, Feet of Clay

1. *TIPS*, April 1988, p. 11.
2. Foster Bailey, *Things to Come* (London: Lucius Press, 1974). Cited in Marrs, *Dark Secrets*, p. 252.
3. Wertham, *The German Euthanasia Program*, p. 52.
4. *Ibid.,* pp. 35-40.
5. *Ibid.,* pp. 43, 51.
6. Wolfensberger, "Extermination of Handicapped People," *op. cit.*
7. Wertham, *The German Euthanasia Program*, pp. 17, 18, 20.
8. *Ibid.,* pp. 33, 34.
9. *Ibid.,* pp. 53, 54.
10. Mendelsohn, *Confessions*, pp. 249, 250.
11. *Ibid.,* pp. 207, 208.
12. Cited in *ibid.,* p. 176.
13. David Holzman, "The Sickly Side of Hospital Stays," *Insight*, February 1, 1988, pp. 48, 49.

CHAPTER 17: Servants of All

1. Texe Marrs documents numerous instances of this in *Dark Secrets of the New Age*, pp. 217-228.

2. John J. Pitney, Jr., "What Jesse Really Wants," *Reason*, July 1988, p. 37. The writer was criticizing presidential aspirant Jesse Jackson's demand for a program of "universal and comprehensive health care" with "cradle-to-grave protection." He rightly points out that this would not lead to greater medical services, but a tendency for government to decide *who* gets medical services—as is true in other countries with socialized medicine.

CHAPTER 18: *Blessed Are the Merciful*

1. Anne L. Austin, *History of Nursing Source Book* (New York: G. P. Putnam's Sons, 1957), p. 39.
2. *Ibid.*, p. 67.
3. *Ibid.*, p. 303.
4. *Ibid.*, p. 304.
5. Malvina W. Keller, *History of the St. Luke's Training School for Nurses* (New York: St. Luke's Hospital, 1938), pp. 9-12. Cited in Austin, *History of Nursing*, p. 418.
6. "Report of Committee on the Training of Nurses," *Transactions of the American Medical Association*, 1869, pp. 161-174. Cited in Austin, *History of Nursing*, p. 430.
7. Wolfensberger, "Extermination of Handicapped People," *op. cit.*
8. Thomas Levinson, "The Heart of the Matter," *Discover*, February 1985.
9. Charles W. Norris, M.D., "Abortion Decision Opened the Door," *Oregonian*, April 13, 1987.
10. "Group Bucks Trend in Feeding-Tube Debate," *World*, April 4, 1988, p. 10.

INDEX